Beginner-Friendly Recipes for Delicious, Creative Bakes
with Minimal Shaping and No Kneading

Easy EVERYDAY SOURDOUGH ★ Bread Baking

Elaine Boddy

Author of *Whole Grain Sourdough at Home* and *The Sourdough Whisperer*

PAGE STREET
PUBLISHING CO.

PAGE STREET
PUBLISHING CO.

First published in 2023 by

Page Street Publishing Co.

27 Congress Street, Suite 1511

Salem, MA 01970

www.pagestreetpublishing.com

Distributed by Macmillan, sales in Canada by The Canadian Manda Group.

26   25   24   23   22   1   2   3   4   5

ISBN-13: 978-1-64567-901-1

ISBN-10: 1-64567-901-2

Library of Congress Control Number: 2022944331

Cover and book design by Katie Beasley for Page Street Publishing Co.
Photography by James Kennedy

Printed and bound in China

I dedicate this book to everyone who has ever baked one of my recipes xx

Contents

Introduction

Hello lovely bakers!

Welcome to my sourdough world. This book brings together so many things that I love: making sourdough as simply as possible; using a sourdough starter in as many ways as possible; and utilizing equipment and ingredients that can be readily found in most kitchens. Let me explain . . . .

Sourdough is truly a simple beast that has been made to look complicated. I am here to undo all of that and promise you that it is far simpler to make than you may think. I ensure that my recipes are uncomplicated, without unnecessary jargon or steps, and are accessible to everyone who would like to make wonderful, tasty, homemade bread of their own.

The recipes in this book are therefore designed so that sourdough bakers of all levels can make them, whether you are a beginner or have had more experience with making sourdough. The book, although not a beginner's guide to making sourdough, includes as much detail as possible in the recipes to ensure that if you are brand-new to sourdough, they will not be daunting.

The methods all utilize my simple, straightforward ways of making sourdough, from easy first mixes to building up the dough by performing pulls and folds on it (see the next section on page 9 for more details). In addition, many use my typical overnight proof to fully develop the dough.

I have listened to hundreds of home bakers around the world and taken on board the elements of sourdough baking that they enjoy and tried to help with the parts of the process they struggle with the most. In this book, you will find an entirely new collection of recipes that have been specifically designed for ease and workable timings. They all use the tins, pans and baking sheets we already have in our kitchens in new and creative ways. This gives us a chance to get more uses out of the items we already own, while providing the added benefit of giving the doughs built-in shaping support and removing the difficulties many bakers have when it comes to shaping doughs.

The recipes also utilize flours and ingredients that are typical in home kitchens, or are easily accessible, and show how sourdough breads can be made in different shapes and forms, as well as be bursting with a variety of flavors and textures.

I hope you enjoy my recipes, and for more ideas, hints and tips, check out my previous books, *Whole Grain Sourdough at Home* and *The Sourdough Whisperer*.

Happy baking!

Elaine
x   x

My Top Tips for Sourdough Success

These are my top tips and helpful hints to ensure you have success with the recipes in this book. From all the questions I have ever been asked and the guidance and assistance I have given sourdough bakers all over the world, these are the pointers that are the absolute keys to being a happy sourdough baker.

The recipes in this book are simple and great for beginner sourdough bakers. However, if you do not have a starter or have never baked a loaf of sourdough before, I recommend you visit my blog where you can find detailed step-by-step instructions and photographs to build a starter and to bake your first loaf: foodbodsourdough.com. You can also get one or both of my previous books that share my master recipe and many other tips and tricks for beginners.

Look After Your Starter

Our sourdough starters are pivotal in our sourdough success. If they do not perform well, our doughs, and therefore our bakes, will not work well, so it is important to keep your starter healthy and strong. Get to know your starter, take note of how it looks and smells and behaves when it is working well so that you will know if anything changes. And if anything does change, take action accordingly.

A healthy active white flour starter has a consistency like thick pancake batter. It grows and doubles several hours after feeding it with flour and water, and may have a bubbly surface and bubbles throughout.

A healthy, active whole-grain starter will be textured and aromatic. It will be thicker than a white starter, and will not break out in a bubbly surface. It will grow in the same way and be full of texture throughout the mix.

Time and temperature are key factors when making sourdough, and I have added tips in the coming sections regarding how they affect dough, but it is also relevant to our starters, too. When it is cold, starters will take longer to respond and become active after feeding. In this instance, allow your starter more time, or place it somewhere warm for a short while. If you put it in a warm place or it is warm in your kitchen (such as during the summer), please keep a close eye on it. Heat will make starters respond faster, and as a result they can easily work too fast and become thin. When a starter becomes thin, or a white flour starter has teeny tiny bubbles all over the surface, it has also become weak. If this happens, feed it more flour than water and bring it back to its thicker consistency to build the body in your starter again and make it stronger. Repeat this as often as you need to to keep your starter strong. But the key here is to keep in mind how temperature can affect a starter's behavior; you can learn a lot just by observing the starter's behavior over time.

Keep your starter in a glass container with a fitted lid to prevent contamination. I use Weck 744 jars for my starter. These jars hold a maximum of 580 ml (20 ounces),, which is also a perfect size; it can be tempting to keep a lot of starter but an ideal base amount is 50 to 100 grams (¼ to ½ cup) to keep your starter fit and healthy. By using this size jar, it prevents the temptation to keep unnecessary starter.

In between uses, store your starter in the fridge; this will effectively put your starter to sleep and protect it until you want to use it again. And when you do, take it from the fridge, feed it and use it once it has responded and grown. It is not necessary to feed your starter in between uses, only when you want to use it to make dough.

Choose Good Flour

To ensure a healthy starter, I always recommend feeding it with good-quality flour. If your starter is a white flour starter, feed it with strong white bread flour for best results. A "strong" flour has a higher level of gluten protein than other flours, such as all-purpose/plain flour, making it perfect for your starter.

A strong flour is also a perfect base flour for making sourdough. Making dough for sourdough includes needing to stretch and pull the dough, plus a long proofing time, and the best flour to withstand both of those elements needs 12 to 13 percent protein.

If you have a limited selection of flours, keep the best-quality one for your starter.

For bakers in the U.S., I recommend King Arthur® bread flour. For those in the U.K., I recommend Matthews Cotswold Flour strong white bread flour. In other countries, look for a good-quality flour with the words "strong" or "bread flour" on the pack.

Top Tip: In my recipes I typically use less salt than you may find in other sourdough recipes. This is based on my personal preference; if you would prefer to use more salt, please feel free to increase the amount.

Perform Pulls and Folds on Your Dough

A key part of making dough for successful sourdough loaves is the pulling and folding action. These stretches of the dough give the gluten a workout, distribute the starter more evenly throughout the mixture and build up the structure in the dough. To perform these, pick up a small portion of the dough from one side of the bowl and literally pull it upward and fold it right across the bowl of dough to the other side. Turn the bowl a few degrees and repeat the actions, over and over, until the dough comes into a smooth or almost smooth ball. Each recipe will state how many sets of these are necessary and if the dough will come into a firm ball or not.

Once the dough comes into a ball, stop, re-cover the bowl and leave the dough to rest until the next actions are required.

Use a Digital Scale

I highly recommend using a digital scale for sourdough making. It is crucial for being able to weigh equal quantities of flour and water when feeding your starter and keeping it strong. A scale will also enable you to weigh the ingredients for your doughs, which will give the best opportunity for success.

If you prefer to use volumes rather than weights, all my recipes include volume measurements. The digital scale I use is made by Salter®.

Use the Mixing Bowl to Measure Your Dough's Growth

Proofing dough and knowing when it is ready to use can be a minefield for sourdough bakers. A really simple way of measuring your dough and knowing if it has grown sufficiently is by using a bowl that is the ideal size to measure the expansion and remove the guesswork. I always use the same bowls for my doughs and they provide the perfect guide.

My bowls are 9 inches (23 cm) in diameter and 3½ inches (9 cm) deep and are made of glass. (Dough sticks less to glass, plus you get the joy of seeing the bubbly dough through the glass.)

If you make my standard size dough (using 500 g [4 cups] of flour), look for the dough to rise and become almost level with the top of the bowl. This is a fully proofed dough. If you make one of my baby doughs (using 300 g [2½ cups] of flour), look for the proofed dough to fill two-thirds of the bowl. When my doughs have proofed and grown almost level with the top edge of these bowls, with a smooth, slightly upwardly domed surface, I know they are fully proofed.

The bowls I use are made by Duralex®. I get my bowls from EcoBakerUK in the U.K. or you can find them online from Shana's Sourdough in the U.S.

Buy a Room Thermometer for Your Kitchen

The biggest threat to sourdough success is the weather. Changes in temperature can affect the proofing time and the behavior of your dough and therefore the outcome of your bakes.

In simple terms: Cold will slow down the proofing, heat will speed it up. And both make a difference.

By having a thermometer in your kitchen and noting the action of your dough and the room temperature at the time, you will be able to build a picture of how dough behaves in your kitchen. This is the most useful thing you can possibly do when making sourdough and makes all the difference in my sourdough baking. By using the size mixing bowl that I recommend in conjunction with a thermometer and keeping these notes, you will be on the path to absolute success with your sourdough making.

The thermometer I use is made by ThermoPro and available online. It shows room temperature and humidity, but also can measure the highest and lowest room temperature across a set period of time, which I find really helpful for making successful sourdough.

As a rough guide, when it is cold, add an extra hour of proofing for every 2°F (1°C) less than 64°F (18°C).

As soon as temperatures begin to regularly exceed 70°F (22°C) overnight, reduce the amount of starter in your dough by half to be able to continue to proof it on the counter overnight. Or switch to a same-day process; that way, you can watch it and avoid overproofing, as the dough will proof faster under the warmer conditions.

Be Firm with Your Dough

After the main/overnight proof, sometimes called the "bulk ferment" or "bulk proof," when the time comes to pull the dough together for the next stage of the process, there can often be fear when handling the dough. Bakers worry about knocking out the bubbles or aeration and consequently can be too timid with the dough at this point. This results in a soft dough that spreads when it is turned out to bake.

It is important at this point to be firm with the dough. Pull it together firmly. A well-made, well-structured, strong dough will withstand whatever you do to it. It will bounce back and grow beautifully as it bakes.

Be firm and be brave—your dough will thank you for it.

Use Bannetons with Rice Flour for Shaping the Dough

For free-form loaves, such as some of those in the Bread Pan and Cake Tin sections, the dough is placed into bannetons, which are baskets that are used to shape the dough before baking. I like using wood pulp bannetons, often called "brotform" bannetons, as they work so well, and I recommend sprinkling the inside of the bannetons with rice flour before placing the dough into them to prevent it from sticking. If you do not have a banneton, use a same-size bowl lined with a clean tea towel sprinkled with rice flour. If you do not have access to rice flour, ground semolina is a perfect alternative.

I use brotform bannetons and I get mine from EcoBakerUK in the U.K. or Shana's Sourdough in the U.S.

Do Not Skip Time in the Fridge

If a recipe includes a period of time for the dough to spend in the fridge, sometimes called the "cold retard," it is there for a reason and I recommend resisting any temptation to skip it. This is an important step for the dough to develop flavor and, most important, to firm up so that when you come to turn it out to bake it, it holds its shape.

The dough will typically grow again in the fridge, but it does not need to. If yours has not, do not fear, it only needs to grow in the oven.

Score Deeply

For free-form loaves that need to be scored prior to baking, score your dough with a thin, sharp blade, preferably a razor blade, and score into the dough about ⅓ inch (1 cm) deep. Scoring the dough encourages it to grow and open up as it bakes.

If your dough seems to collapse once scored, again, do not fear. If it is a well-made, strong dough it will grow and bake perfectly.

I use a lame to score my dough; a lame is simply the term for a wooden handle that holds the razor blade. My lames are handmade by The Garlic Tun.

Loaves baked in loaf tins do not need to be scored.

Wait

Once they are baked, place the full loaves on a cooling rack and wait at least 1 hour before slicing into them. I know this can be a challenge but it really is worth it. If you slice into your carefully created loaf too soon, it will still be cooking inside, which will make it gummy and sticky to eat. Waiting really does bring out the best in your loaf.

Timetables

Each recipe in the book is designed to be made to a certain timetable. Some are overnight recipes, some are same-day and some are fast and immediate. The overnight and same-day recipes can be interchanged; to do so please note the differences in the amount of starter and water used and the proofing information. Apart from the starter and water, the rest of the ingredients can be swapped between the recipes.

Use a Mixer

The first mix of the doughs in the following recipes can be done in a stand mixer. Where the recipe directions say to place all the dough ingredients into your mixing bowl, place them instead into the bowl of your stand mixer. Mix on a low speed for 4 to 5 minutes. Remove the dough and place it into your usual, free-standing mixing bowl. The doughs need to still be stretched and pulled to build them up, so I recommend moving the doughs to your mixing bowl after the first mix. This will also help with judging the proof, as noted previously.

Always Bake Your Dough

If your proofed dough does not look or feel like you expected it to, never throw it away. Always bake it. Dough can always be used. If the dough was going to be baked into a free-form/free-standing loaf but you fear the dough is too soft to hold its shape, use one of my sandwich loaf recipe processes as your guide from step 5 onward, and bake the dough in a tin. If the dough is excessively bubbly and slack and you fear it has overproofed, stir in some milk and use it to make pancakes, or stir in some yogurt and use the mix for flatbreads.

Never Forget . . .

Sourdough is endlessly forgiving and starters are very resilient. Do not immediately fear the worst; there is always a way to use or boost them.

Find a lot more help, hints, tips and answers to every question you will ever have about sourdough in my previous book, *The Sourdough Whisperer*.

The Bread Pan COLLECTION

Easy-to-Handle Doughs for
Classic Crusty Loaves and More

If you are a sourdough maker or home cook, you may already own a large Dutch oven, enamel roaster or some other pan for baking your loaves. In this section, you will find a collection of recipes baked in these pans, providing more uses for these pans and giving the dough the benefit of being baked in a pan with a lid and a closed environment. This captures the steam from the dough and helps boost the growth of the dough as it bakes.

I use a 10-inch (26-cm)-diameter enamel pan for all my free-form sourdough baking. These recipes can also be made with an oval banneton and pan. The oval pan I use is 12 inches (30 cm) long.

Easy Shape Crusty White Loaf

This recipe will give you the archetypal crusty, round sourdough loaf. For this version, I use my renowned master recipe, the original of which is available online and in my previous cookbooks, which I tweaked to produce a firm and easy-to-handle dough to ensure a successful round loaf every time. The dough will come together easily and not be challenging to shape and work with.

Note that if this is your first time baking a loaf of sourdough, I would recommend you visit my blog to find detailed, step-by-step instructions and photographs to build a starter and bake your first loaf: foodbodsourdough.com.

Equipment: A round banneton, 8 inches (22 cm) in diameter and 3¼ inches (8.5 cm) deep, or a cloth-lined bowl dusted with rice flour. Set aside a medium-sized baking pan lined with parchment paper, plus a lid. My pan is a 10-inch (26-cm)-diameter enamel roaster pan.

Makes 1 standard loaf

50 g (¼ cup) active starter

325 g (1⅓ cups) water

500 g (4 cups) strong white bread flour

7 g (1 tsp) salt, or to taste

Rice flour, for dusting

Step 1: In the early evening, in a large mixing bowl, roughly mix together all the ingredients, except the rice flour, until you have a shaggy, rough dough. Cover the bowl with a clean shower cap or your choice of cover and leave the bowl on the counter for 2 hours.

Step 2: After 2 hours, perform the first set of pulls and folds until the dough feels less sticky and comes together into a firm, smooth ball. Cover the bowl again and leave it on your counter.

Step 3: After 1 to 1½ hours, do one more set of pulls and folds on the dough, covering the dough again afterward. Let it rest again for another hour, then do one more set of pulls and folds, then cover the bowl again.

Step 4: Leave the covered bowl on the counter overnight, typically 8 to 10 hours, at 64 to 68°F (18 to 20°C).

Step 5: In the morning, you should be greeted by a bowl full of grown dough. Perform a set of pulls and folds to firmly pull the dough into a nice ball that holds its shape. Place your hand over the whole dough and lift it into the banneton, smooth side down. Sprinkle extra rice flour down the sides and over the top of the dough. Cover the banneton and place it in the fridge for 3 to 24 hours.

Step 6: When you are ready to bake, decide whether you would like to bake it in a preheated oven or from a cold start. If preheating, set the oven to 425°F (220°C) convection or 450°F (230°C) conventional.

(continued)

Easy Shape Crusty White Loaf (Continued)

Remove the cover from the banneton, then place the parchment paper over the top of the banneton and put the pan upside down over the top of them both. With one hand under the banneton and one on the pan, turn it all over together to turn the dough out of the banneton and into the pan. Score the dome of dough.

Step 7: If you preheated the oven, put the lid on the pan and bake it for 50 minutes. If you are using a cold start, place the covered pan of dough in the oven, set the temperature as above and set a timer for 55 minutes.

After the baking time, remove the pan from the oven. Open the lid and check the loaf. If you feel that it is looking pale, place the pan with the loaf back into the hot oven, minus the lid, for 5 to 10 minutes to brown the loaf to the color of your choice.

Step 8: Once it is baked, carefully remove the loaf from the pan, saving the parchment paper for next time, and allow the baked loaf to cool on a wire rack for at least an hour before slicing.

Top Tip: If you feel confident handling dough or if your dough feels dry at any point, your flour may need more water, in which case add 25 grams (⅛ cup) of water to the dough.

Same-Day Chia Seed Boule

This recipe will enable you to make a loaf from scratch within a day, while also using more water than other loaves. However, do not fear a "higher hydration" dough. The chia seeds will soak up some of the water and help to make this a very easy-to-manipulate dough, while producing a perfectly round baked loaf. This loaf is also made using a portion of whole wheat flour that will assist in making this a manageable dough while also enhancing the sourdough flavor.

Equipment: A round banneton, 8 inches (22 cm) in diameter and 3¼ inches (8.5 cm) deep, or a cloth-lined bowl dusted with rice flour. Set aside a medium-sized baking pan lined with parchment paper, plus a lid. My pan is a 10-inch (26-cm)-diameter enamel roaster pan.

Location: Use a warm place to proof the dough. I use my oven with the pilot light on and the door propped open, which creates an even temperature of 77°F (25°C). Alternatively, use a proofing box.

Makes 1 standard loaf

100 g (½ cup) active starter

375 g (1¾ cups) warm water, around 100°F (38°C)

400 g (3¼ cups) strong white bread flour

100 g (¾ cup) whole wheat flour

50 g (¼ cup) chia seeds

7 g (1 tsp) salt, or to taste

Rice flour, for dusting

Step 1: In the morning, using a medium-sized mixing bowl, roughly mix together all the ingredients, except the rice flour, until you have a shaggy, rough dough. The dough will be sticky. Cover the bowl with a clean shower cap or your choice of cover and leave the bowl in your chosen warm spot for 30 minutes.

Step 2: After 30 minutes, perform the first set of pulls and folds, until the dough feels less sticky and comes together into a soft ball. This will be a warm and soft seed-speckled dough. Cover the bowl again and place it back in the warmth.

Step 3: After half an hour, perform the next set of pulls and folds, repeating the same actions again; the dough should be warm and stretchy, and it should come together into an easy ball. Place the covered bowl back in the warmth.

Step 4: After another half an hour, perform the last set of pulls and folds; the dough should come together into a nice, bouncy ball. Place the covered bowl back in the warmth for the next 3 hours, or until the dough has doubled in size.

(continued)

Step 5: Once the dough is double its original size—it may be soft from the warm proofing—perform one last set of pulls and folds to firmly pull the dough into a nice ball. Place your hand over the whole dough and lift it into the banneton, smooth side down. Sprinkle extra rice flour down the sides and over the top of the dough. Cover the banneton and place it in the fridge for at least 1 hour. It should now be early afternoon and you can decide whether you would like to bake the loaf for late afternoon or early evening.

Step 6: When you are ready to bake, decide whether you would like to bake in a preheated oven or from a cold start. If preheating, set the oven to 425°F (220°C) convection or 450°F (230°C) conventional.

Remove the cover from the banneton, then place the parchment paper over the top of the banneton and put the pan upside down over the top of them both. With one hand under the banneton and one on the pan, turn it all over together to turn the dough out of the banneton and into the pan. Score the dome of dough.

Step 7: If you preheated the oven, put the lid on the pan and bake it for 50 minutes. If you are using a cold start, place the covered pan of dough in the oven, set the temperature as above and set a timer for 55 minutes.

Remove the lid or cover 10 minutes before the end of the baking time.

After the full baking time, remove the pan from the oven. If you feel that it is looking pale, place the pan with the loaf back in the hot oven, minus the lid, for 5 to 10 minutes to brown the loaf to the color of your choice.

Step 8: Once it is baked, carefully remove the loaf from the pan, saving the parchment paper for next time, and allow the baked loaf to cool on a wire rack for at least an hour before slicing.

Easy Shape Seeded Boule

Adding seeds to doughs is one of my favorite variations. My entire family enjoys the added flavor and crunch, plus adding seeds has the benefit of creating a firm dough that is easy to handle and shape. I use pumpkin seeds in this loaf, but you can use your favorite seeds or a mix of them.

Equipment: A round banneton, 8 inches (22 cm) in diameter and 3¼ inches (8.5 cm) deep, or a cloth-lined bowl dusted with rice flour. Set aside a medium-sized baking pan lined with parchment paper, plus a lid. My pan is a 10-inch (26-cm)-diameter enamel roaster pan.

Makes 1 standard loaf

50 g (¼ cup) active starter

350 g (1½ cups) water

500 g (4 cups) strong white bread flour

75 g (½ cup) pumpkin seeds

7 g (1 tsp) salt, or to taste

Rice flour, for dusting

Step 1: In the early evening, in a large mixing bowl, roughly mix together all the ingredients, except the rice flour, until you have a shaggy, rough dough. Cover the bowl with a clean shower cap or your choice of cover and leave the bowl on the counter for 2 hours.

Step 2: After this time, perform the first set of pulls and folds on the dough until it comes into a soft, seed-studded ball. You will be able to feel the seeds throughout the dough. Cover the bowl again and leave it on your counter.

Step 3: After 1 to 1½ hours, do one more set of pulls and folds on the dough, covering the dough again afterward. Let it rest for another hour, then do one more set of pulls and folds and cover the bowl again.

Step 4: Leave the covered bowl on the counter overnight, typically 8 to 10 hours, at 64 to 68°F (18 to 20°C).

Step 5: In the morning, you should be greeted by a bowl full of grown dough. Perform a set of pulls and folds to firmly pull the dough into a nice ball that holds its shape. Place your hand over the whole dough and lift it into the banneton, smooth side down. Sprinkle extra rice flour down the sides and over the top of the dough. Cover the banneton and place it in the fridge for 3 to 24 hours.

Step 6: When you are ready to bake, decide whether you would like to bake in a preheated oven or from a cold start. If preheating, set the oven to 425°F (220°C) convection or 450°F (230°C) conventional.

Remove the cover from the banneton, then place the parchment paper over the top of the banneton and put the pan upside down over the top of them both. With one hand under the banneton and one on the pan, turn it all over together to turn the dough out of the banneton and into the pan. Score the dome of dough.

Step 7: If you preheated the oven, put the lid on the pan and bake it for 50 minutes. If you are using a cold start, place the covered pan of dough in the oven, set the temperature as above and set a timer for 55 minutes.

After the baking time, remove the pan from the oven. Open the lid and check the loaf. If you feel that it is looking pale, place the pan with the loaf back in the hot oven, minus the lid, for 5 to 10 minutes to brown the loaf to the color of your choice.

Step 8: Once it is baked, carefully remove the loaf from the pan, saving the parchment paper for next time, and allow the baked loaf to cool on a wire rack for at least an hour before slicing.

Yogurt and Nut Boule

The addition of yogurt in sourdough produces an extra sour flavor in the baked loaf, while also giving the benefit of making a firm dough that renders it manageable and simple to shape. The addition of nuts adds texture to the dough as well as nutty goodness. I use walnuts and they produce pretty pink streaks in the baked loaf.

Equipment: A round banneton, 8 inches (22 cm) in diameter and 3¼ inches (8.5 cm) deep, or a cloth-lined bowl dusted with rice flour. Set aside a medium-sized baking pan lined with parchment paper, plus a lid. My pan is a 10-inch (26-cm)-diameter enamel roaster pan.

Makes 1 standard loaf

50 g (¼ cup) active starter

225 g (scant 1 cup) water

150 g (⅔ cup) plain/natural yogurt

500 g (4 cups) strong white bread flour

75 g (½ cup) hand-crushed walnuts

7 g (1 tsp) salt, or to taste

Rice flour, for dusting

Step 1: In the early evening, in a large mixing bowl, roughly mix together all the ingredients, except the rice flour, until you have a shaggy, rough dough. Cover the bowl with a clean shower cap or your choice of cover and leave the bowl on the counter for 2 hours.

Step 2: After the rest time, perform the first set of pulls and folds. The dough will be stiff and tight and will come into a firm nut-studded ball. Cover the bowl again and leave it on your counter to rest.

Step 3: After 1 to 1½ hours, do one more set of pulls and folds on the dough, covering the dough again afterward. Let it rest for another hour, then do one more set of pulls and folds and cover the bowl again.

Step 4: Leave the covered bowl on the counter overnight, typically 8 to 10 hours, at 64 to 68°F (18 to 20°C).

Step 5: In the morning, you should be greeted by a bowl full of grown dough. Perform a set of pulls and folds to firmly pull the dough into a nice ball that holds its shape. Place your hand over the whole dough and lift it into the banneton, smooth side down. Sprinkle extra rice flour down the sides and over the top of the dough. Cover the banneton and place it in the fridge for 3 to 24 hours.

Top Tip: I broke up my walnuts by hand so that they were in small pieces. You can use any nuts of your choice.

Step 6: When you are ready to bake it, decide whether you would like to bake in a preheated oven or from a cold start. If preheating, set the oven to 425°F (220°C) convection or 450°F (230°C) conventional.

Remove the cover from the banneton, then place the parchment paper over the top of the banneton and put the pan upside down over the top of them both. With one hand under the banneton and one on the pan, turn it all over together to turn the dough out of the banneton and into the pan. Score the dome of dough.

Top Tip: If you would like this loaf to be lighter in density, when you first mix the ingredients add an extra 25 to 50 grams (⅛ to ¼ cup) of water to the dough.

Step 7: If you preheated the oven, put the lid on the pan and bake it for 50 minutes. If you are using a cold start, place the covered pan of dough in the oven, set the temperature as above and set a timer for 55 minutes.

After the baking time, remove the pan from the oven. Open the lid and check the loaf. If you feel that it is looking pale, place the pan with the loaf back in the hot oven, minus the lid, for 5 to 10 minutes to brown the loaf to the color of your choice.

Step 8: Once it is baked, carefully remove the loaf from the pan, saving the parchment paper for next time, and allow the baked loaf to cool on a wire rack for at least an hour before slicing.

Mincemeat, Carrot and Buttermilk Loaf

This loaf came about from a fridge raid, very much like so many of my flavored or filled loaves; however, I love it so much that it has become one of the loaves I have on regular rotation in my kitchen. I always end up with half a jar of mincemeat left over in my fridge after Christmas, so one of the aims of this recipe is to show once again that you can open your fridge, peek in, grab whatever you find and add it to a dough. You may even find that you create a new family favorite this way. Mincemeat is made from apples, dried fruits and spices. If you cannot find it in your local food stores, there are many recipes available online to make your own.

Equipment: A round banneton, 8 inches (22 cm) in diameter and 3¼ inches (8.5 cm) deep, or a cloth-lined bowl dusted with rice flour. Set aside a medium-sized baking pan lined with parchment paper, plus a lid. My pan is a 10-inch (26-cm)-diameter enamel roaster pan.

Makes 1 standard loaf

50 g (¼ cup) active starter

250 g (1 cup) water

75 g (⅓ cup) buttermilk

350 g (2¾ cups) strong white bread flour

150 g (1¼ cups) whole-grain spelt flour

150 g (½ cup) store-bought or homemade mincemeat

100 g (1 cup) grated carrot

7 g (1 tsp) salt, or to taste

Rice flour, for dusting

Step 1: In the early evening, in a large mixing bowl, roughly mix together all the ingredients, except the rice flour, until you have a shaggy, rough dough; this will be a sticky, heavy mix initially. Cover the bowl with a clean shower cap or your choice of cover and leave the bowl on the counter for 2 hours.

Step 2: After the rest time, perform the first set of pulls and folds on the dough; it will be soft and will come into a loose ball. Cover the bowl again and leave it on your counter.

Step 3: During the next few hours, do two more sets of pulls and folds on the dough. With each set the dough will be easier to pull and stretch. Pull the dough into a ball each time, covering the dough after each set. Perform the final set before going to bed.

Step 4: Leave the covered bowl on the counter overnight, typically 8 to 10 hours, at 64 to 68°F (18 to 20°C).

Step 5: In the morning, you should be greeted by a bowl full of grown dough. Perform a set of pulls and folds to firmly pull the dough into a nice ball that holds its shape. Place your hand over the whole dough and lift it into the banneton, smooth side down. Sprinkle extra rice flour down the sides and over the top of the dough. Cover the banneton and place it in the fridge for 3 to 24 hours.

(continued)

Mincemeat, Carrot and Buttermilk Loaf (Continued)

Step 6: When you are ready to bake, decide whether you would like to bake in a preheated oven or from a cold start. If preheating, set the oven to 425°F (220°C) convection or 450°F (230°C) conventional.

Remove the cover from the banneton, then place the parchment paper over the top of the banneton and put the pan upside down over the top of them both. With one hand under the banneton and one on the pan, turn it all over together to turn the dough out of the banneton and into the pan. Score the dough.

Step 7: If you preheated the oven, put the lid on and bake it for 50 minutes. If you are using a cold start, place the covered pan of dough in the oven, set the temperature as above and set a timer for 55 minutes.

After the baking time for either option, remove the covered pan from the oven. Open the lid to check the loaf. If you feel that your loaf is looking pale, place it back in the hot oven, in its pan, minus the lid, for 5 to 10 minutes to brown the loaf to the color of your choice. This loaf will bake to a darker color than a typical loaf, due to the whole-grain spelt flour, the buttermilk and the sugars in the mincemeat.

Step 8: Once it is baked, carefully remove the loaf from the pan, saving the parchment paper for next time, and allow the baked loaf to cool on a wire rack for at least an hour before slicing. Your kitchen will smell wonderful!

Top Tips: If you do not have whole-grain spelt flour, replace it with the same amount of whole wheat flour.

If you cannot find mincemeat or would prefer not to make any, use 75 grams (½ cup) of apricot jam and 75 grams (½ cup) of mixed dried fruits.

If you do not have buttermilk on hand, mix 250 grams (1 cup) of milk with 20 grams (1 tbsp) of white vinegar or lemon juice, stir them well and allow it to sit briefly until it curdles and thickens up.

Same-Day Easy Shape Pizza

How do you fancy some supremely tasty, wonderfully textured sourdough pizza bases, made from start to finish in one day, with an easy-to-shape dough that is ready for all your favorite toppings? That is what this recipe will give you. The timings allow you to make the dough in the morning and bake the pizzas by the evening, or to bake the bases and have them ready for another time. By baking the bases in your bread pan, the pan shapes them for you! Since devising it, I use this process a lot in my kitchen now and my boys always give the pizzas a thumbs-up.

Equipment: I use my 10-inch (26-cm)-diameter enamel roaster pan; you can use your roaster, Dutch oven or a large, round, covered pan of a similar size. Line your choice with good-quality parchment paper.

Location: Use a warm place to proof the dough. I use my oven with the pilot light on and the door propped open, which creates an even temperature of 77°F (25°C). Alternatively, use a proofing box.

Makes 2 medium-sized pizzas

60 g (¼ cup plus 1 tbsp) active starter

200 g (¾ cup) warm water, around 100°F (38°C)

300 g (2½ cups) strong white bread flour, plus more for dusting

4 g (½ tsp) salt, or to taste

Optional Toppings (per pizza)

100 g (½ cup) tomato sauce or basil pesto

125 g (1 cup) sliced fresh mozzarella

Step 1: In a medium-sized mixing bowl, roughly mix together all the ingredients, except the toppings, until you have a shaggy, rough dough. The dough will be sticky. Cover the bowl with a clean shower cap or your choice of cover and leave the bowl in your chosen warm spot for half an hour.

Step 2: After half an hour, perform the first set of pulls and folds; this will be a warm, soft dough. Cover the bowl again and place it back in the warmth.

Step 3: After another half an hour, perform the next set of pulls and folds. The dough should be nice and stretchy and bouncy, and it should come together into a nice, smooth, soft ball. Place the covered bowl back in the warmth.

Step 4: After another 30 minutes, perform the last set of pulls and folds; the dough should come together into a nice, smooth, bouncy ball. Place the covered bowl back in the warmth for the next 3 hours, or until the dough has doubled in size.

(continued)

Same-Day Easy Shape Pizza (Continued)

Step 5: Once the dough is double its original size, using a bowl scraper or your hands, split the dough roughly in half while still in the bowl and place one half into your lined pan. I find the dough plops happily and unceremoniously into the pan, which is perfect.

Either cover the remaining dough again, or place it into another pan if you have two. If you do not have two pans, place the second portion of dough back into your bowl, cover it and place it in the fridge to use later. You can also bake it immediately on a baking sheet using the focaccia process as described on page 32. For the dough you are working with now, place the lid on your pan and allow the dough to proof again and spread across the base of the pan, for 1 to 2 hours at room temperature. Once it has relaxed and spread, wet your fingertips and use them to push the dough out to the edges of the inside of the pan.

Step 6: When you are ready to bake, decide whether you would like to bake in a preheated oven or from a cold start. If preheating, set the oven to 400°F (200°C) convection or 425°F (220°C) conventional.

Step 7: If you preheated the oven, place the lid on the pan and bake it for 20 minutes. If you are using a cold start, place the covered pan of dough in the oven, set the temperature as above and set a timer for 25 minutes. After this time, carefully remove the pizza base from the pan, remove the paper and either allow it to cool to use later, or add the toppings of your choice and return it to the oven—directly onto the oven shelf—to bake for 10 to 15 minutes, or until the cheese has fully melted.

Step 8: Once the pizza has baked, remove it from the oven and serve it. If you saved the second portion of dough to bake in the same pan, take the bowl of dough from the fridge and let it come up to room temperature—I typically leave mine for about an hour—at the same time allowing the pan to cool down, and follow the steps from step 5 onward to proof and bake it.

Top Tip: If you choose to use the baked base later, add your toppings and bake it for 12 to 15 minutes in a preheated oven, or 15 to 18 minutes from a cold start, or until the cheese is melted and browned and the base is cooked and crisp.

Milk Dinner Rolls

These light and fluffy rolls are perfect not just for dinner, but also breakfast, lunch—or any event, really! The milk powder adds a softness to the rolls and baking them in a covered pan encourages them to rise like clouds before removing the lid to brown them. Once they are baked, spread them with butter and let it melt all over the hot rolls to give them an alluring shine.

Equipment: I use my 10-inch (26-cm)-diameter enamel roaster pan; you can use your roaster, Dutch oven or a large, round, covered pan of a similar size. Line your choice with good-quality parchment paper.

Makes 12 kissing rolls

50 g (¼ cup) active starter

350 g (1½ cups) water

500 g (4 cups) strong white bread flour

14 g (2 tsp) milk powder

7 g (1 tsp) salt, or to taste

Topping
14 g (1 tbsp) butter, salted or unsalted

Step 1: In the early evening, in a large mixing bowl, roughly mix together all the ingredients, except the butter, leaving the dough shaggy. Cover the bowl with a clean shower cap or your choice of cover and leave it on the counter for 2 hours.

Step 2: After this time, perform the first set of pulls and folds on the dough; it will be sticky at this point but it will come into a soft ball. Cover the bowl and leave it on the counter.

Step 3: After 1 to 1½ hours, do another set of pulls and folds on the dough, covering the dough again afterward. Let it rest again for another hour, do one more set of pulls and folds and then cover the bowl again. The dough will be nicely stretchy and will easily come together into a soft ball each time.

Step 4: Leave the covered bowl on the counter overnight, typically 8 to 10 hours, at 64 to 68°F (18 to 20°C).

Step 5: The next morning, place the dough, untouched but still covered, in the fridge for at least an hour, until you are ready to use it (this could be for lunch, dinner or breakfast the next day). In the fridge, the dough will firm up, making it easier to work with later.

When you are ready to shape the rolls, turn the dough out onto a floured surface. Using a dough knife, cut the dough into twelve pieces, each 75 grams (2½ oz), and shape each piece into a small firm ball. Place the balls into the lined base of the bread pan, evenly spaced apart, cover the pan with its lid and allow them to proof again for 1½ to 2 hours until they have doubled in size and are touching one another.

Alternatively, place the covered pan in the fridge for up to 24 hours and allow the rolls to proof again slowly until you are ready to bake. When you are ready to bake, bake the rolls directly from the fridge—they do not need to sit at room temperature before baking.

Top Tip: If you do not have milk powder, use 175 grams (¾ cup) of water and 175 grams (¾ cup) of milk of your choice.

Step 6: When you are ready to bake, decide whether you would like to bake in a preheated oven or from a cold start. If preheating, set the oven to 400°F (200°C) convection or 425°F (220°C) conventional.

Step 7: If you preheated the oven, bake the rolls, covered, for 25 minutes, or until they are nicely risen and starting to brown.

To bake from a cold start, place the covered pan of dough in the oven, set the temperature as directed and bake them for a total of 30 minutes, or until they are nicely risen and browning. After this time, remove the lid and bake them for a further 5 minutes to brown.

Step 8: Once they are baked, remove them from the oven and place the round of rolls, still intact, onto a rack, and spread the butter all over the top, allowing it to melt as you spread it. Eat them once they are slightly cooled.

Oil-Free Focaccia

Focaccia is a wonderfully airy, flat bread, typically made with lots of olive oil. I have been asked many times if it can be made without the oil, so I give you this oil-free version. This bread is also baked into the base of the pan I usually use to bake my sourdough loaves in, giving the pan another use in our baking, while at the same time providing bakers with easy shaping as the dough takes on the shape of the base of the pan.

Equipment: I use my 10-inch (26-cm)-diameter enamel roaster pan; you can use your roaster, Dutch oven or a large, round, covered pan of a similar size. Line your choice with good-quality parchment paper.

Makes 1 standard loaf

30 g (⅛ cup) active starter

250 g (1 cup) water

300 g (2½ cups) strong white bread flour

4 g (½ tsp) salt, or to taste

Step 1: In the early evening, in a large mixing bowl, roughly mix together all the ingredients, until you have a shaggy, rough dough. Cover the bowl with a clean shower cap or your choice of cover and leave the bowl on the counter for 2 hours.

Step 2: After the 2-hour rest, perform the first set of pulls and folds on the dough until it feels less sticky and comes together into a soft ball. It will be soft, sticky and stretchy and the ball of dough will not hold its shape. Cover the bowl again and leave it on your counter.

Step 3: After another 1 to 2 hours, do another set of pulls and folds on the dough, covering the dough again once completed.

Step 4: Leave the covered bowl on the counter overnight, typically 8 to 10 hours, at 64 to 68°F (18 to 20°C).

Step 5: The next morning, the dough will have doubled in size and will be ready to be used to make focaccia. Either use the dough immediately, or place the bowl, untouched and still covered, in the fridge until you want to use it. If you store it in the fridge, a few hours before you want to bake the focaccia, remove the bowl from the fridge, allow it an hour on the counter to let the dough come up to room temperature and continue.

Using a bowl scraper or your hands, gently ease the bubbly risen dough from the bowl into the lined pan and put on the lid. The dough will be an unformed blob of dough in the pan at this point; it will not have any shape yet. Leave it on the counter for 2 to 3 hours. The dough will now loosen and spread slightly.

Step 6: When you are ready to bake it, decide whether you would like to bake in a preheated oven or from a cold start. If preheating, set the oven to 400°F (200°C) convection or 425°F (220°C) conventional.

Top Tip: After baking, this bread can be wrapped or frozen until a later date. This focaccia is delicious in its simple form, or you can get creative with toppings, such as fresh rosemary, garlic, olives, tomatoes or your favorite choices.

Liberally wet your fingertips and firmly press dimples all over the dough, spreading it out at the same time, until it fills the pan.

Step 7: If you preheated the oven, put the lid on the pan and bake it for 20 minutes. If you are using a cold start, place the pan of dough in the oven, set the temperature as above and set a timer for 25 minutes.

After this time, remove the pan from the oven and carefully remove the bread from the pan, remove the paper and place the round bread directly onto the oven shelf, uncovered, and bake it for a further 5 minutes.

Step 8: Remove the baked focaccia from the oven and let it rest on a rack briefly until you can handle it, cut it into pieces and serve.

Turkish-Style Seed-Topped Pide

This wonderfully light flatbread is brushed with a mixture of egg, yogurt and water and then topped with seeds before baking. This gives the seeds something to stick to and the baked bread its golden color while also adding a crisp finish to the surface of the bread. I use a mixture of white sesame seeds and kalonji/onion seeds over the top, but you can also use white and black sesame seeds. Typically a "pide" has a crisscross pattern on the top, created by using your fingertips, but dimpling will also work.

Equipment: I use my 10-inch (26-cm)-diameter enamel roaster pan; you can use your roaster, Dutch oven or a large, round, covered pan of a similar size. Line your choice with good-quality parchment paper.

Makes 1 standard loaf

30 g (⅛ cup) active starter

200 g (¾ cup) water

30 g (2 tbsp) olive oil

300 g (2½ cups) strong white bread flour

4 g (½ tsp) salt, or to taste

Toppings

1 large egg yolk

15 g (1 tbsp) water

15 g (1 tbsp) plain/natural yogurt

9 g (1 tbsp) white sesame seeds

9 g (1 tbsp) black onion/kalonji seeds

Step 1: In the early evening, in a large mixing bowl, roughly mix together all the ingredients, except the toppings, until you have a shaggy, rough dough. Cover the bowl with a clean shower cap or your choice of cover and leave the bowl on the counter for 2 hours.

Step 2: After the 2 hours, perform the first set of pulls and folds on the dough. This is a small dough and it will feel sticky at this point but will come together into a soft ball. Cover the bowl again and leave it on your counter.

Step 3: After another 1 to 2 hours, do another set of pulls and folds on the dough; it will now be smooth and stretchy. Cover the dough again once completed.

Step 4: Leave the covered bowl on the counter overnight, typically 8 to 10 hours, at 64 to 68°F (18 to 20°C).

Step 5: The next morning, the dough will have doubled in size with a smooth surface, and will now be ready to make your pide. Either use the dough immediately, or place the bowl, untouched and still covered, in the fridge until you want to use it. If you stored it in the fridge, before you want to bake the bread, remove the bowl from the fridge and allow it to sit for 1 hour on the counter to let the dough come up to room temperature.

When you are ready, using the same pulling and folding action, pull the dough into a soft ball and place it smooth side up in the middle of your lined pan. Place the lid on the pan. Leave it on the counter for 2 to 3 hours. The dough will loosen and spread slightly.

Step 6: When you are ready to bake, decide whether you would like to bake in a preheated oven or from a cold start. If preheating, set the oven to 400°F (200°C) convection or 425°F (220°C) conventional.

Wet your fingertips and firmly press the dough out to the edge of the pan so that it fills the base of your bread pan. Using wetted fingers again, press into the dough 1 inch (2.5 cm) from the edge of the dough all the way around to draw a circle in the dough, then use your fingertips to draw lines across the dough within that circle, creating a crisscross pattern. Mix the egg yolk, water and yogurt together well, and brush the mixture over the top of the dough. Sprinkle the seeds on top.

Step 7: If you preheated the oven, put the lid on the pan and bake it for 15 minutes. If you are using a cold start, place the pan of dough in the oven, set the temperature as above and set a timer for 20 minutes.

After this time, take the pan from the oven and carefully remove the bread from the pan, remove the paper and place the round bread directly onto the oven shelf, uncovered, and bake it for a further 10 minutes.

Step 8: Remove the baked pide from the oven and let it rest on a rack briefly until you can handle it, cut it into pieces and serve.

Cheesy Herby Pull Apart Rolls

These pull aparts are soft and light like clouds. I simply cannot describe them any other way but luscious. The herby dough is split into twelve equal pieces, rolled into little balls, then placed in the base of the bread pan and left to proof. Sprinkle them with grated Parmesan, then bake them with the pan lid on and they grow and grow while baking. These are possibly the lightest sourdough rolls I have ever baked.

Equipment: I use my 10-inch (26-cm)-diameter enamel roaster pan; you can use your roaster, Dutch oven or a large, round, covered pan of a similar size. Line your choice with good-quality parchment paper.

Makes 12 kissing rolls

50 g (¼ cup) active starter

325 g (1⅓ cups) water

500 g (4 cups) strong white bread flour

7 g (3½ tsp) dried herbs (I use equal amounts of dried parsley and mint)

7 g (1 tsp) salt, or to taste

Topping
30 g (¼ cup) finely grated Parmesan cheese

Step 1: In the early evening, in a large mixing bowl, roughly mix together all the ingredients, except the Parmesan, leaving the dough shaggy. Cover the bowl with a clean shower cap or your choice of cover and leave it on the counter for 2 hours.

Step 2: After this time, perform the first set of pulls and folds on the dough; it will be sticky at this point, but stretchy and then firm. Cover the bowl and leave it on the counter.

Step 3: After 1 to 1½ hours, do another set of pulls and folds on the dough, covering the dough again afterward. Let it rest again for another hour, then do one more set of pulls and folds, then cover the bowl again. The dough will be nicely stretchy and will easily come together into a firm ball.

Step 4: Leave the covered bowl on the counter overnight, typically 8 to 10 hours, at 64 to 68°F (18 to 20°C).

Step 5: The next morning, place the dough, untouched but still covered, in the fridge for at least an hour, until you are ready to use it. In the fridge, the dough will firm up, making it easier to work with later.

When you are ready to shape the rolls, turn the dough out onto a floured surface. Using a dough knife, cut the dough into twelve pieces, each 75 grams (2½ oz), and shape each piece into a small firm ball. Place the balls into the lined base of the bread pan, evenly spaced apart (in my pan the edges of the balls just touch). Cover the pan with its lid and allow them to proof again for 1½ to 2 hours, or until they have doubled in size and are touching.

Alternatively, place the covered pan in the fridge for up to 24 hours and allow the rolls to proof again slowly until you are ready to bake. When you are ready to bake, bake the rolls directly from the fridge—they do not need to sit at room temperature before baking.

Step 6: When you are ready to bake, decide whether you would like to bake in a preheated oven or from a cold start. If preheating, set the oven to 400°F (200°C) convection or 425°F (220°C) conventional.

Step 7: Sprinkle the Parmesan all over the proofed rolls. Put the pan lid back on. If you preheated the oven, bake the rolls for 25 minutes, or until they are nicely risen and starting to brown.

To bake from a cold start, place the covered pan of dough in the oven, set the temperature as directed and bake them for a total of 30 minutes, or until they are nicely risen and starting to brown. After this time, remove the lid and bake them for a further 5 minutes to brown the cheese.

Step 8: Once they are baked, remove the rolls from the oven and serve them once they are slightly cooled.

Raspberry, Chocolate and Honeycomb Snug Swirls

This pan full of fabulousness takes my enriched dough base and packs it with raspberries, dark chocolate chips and honeycomb pieces. These are irresistible treats, baked snugly in your bread pan to create a round of pull apart rolls that are ideal for sharing, gifting or presenting at any event, or for keeping all to yourself for pure indulgence. The use of frozen raspberries means that they almost "self-sauce" as the rolls are baked, and the chocolate chips and honeycomb pieces can be swapped with whatever takes your fancy.

Equipment: I use my 10-inch (26-cm)-diameter enamel roaster pan; you can use your roaster, Dutch oven or a large, round, covered pan of a similar size. Line your choice with good-quality parchment paper.

Makes 12 filled rolls

100 g (½ cup) active starter

300 g (1 ¼ cups) milk, cold or at room temperature (I use reduced-fat or 2% milk, but you can also use full-fat or whole milk)

1 large egg

50 g (¼ cup) butter (I use slightly salted butter), at room temperature

50 g (¼ cup) runny honey

500 g (4 cups) strong white bread flour

7 g (1 tsp) salt, or to taste

Filling

200 g (1 cup) frozen raspberries, direct from the freezer

50 g (⅓ cup) dark chocolate chips

50 g (¼ cup) honeycomb pieces

Step 1: In the early evening, in a large mixing bowl, roughly mix together all the ingredients, except the fillings. It will be a sticky dough. The butter will not be fully mixed through yet; it will become mixed in fully as you complete the next steps. Cover the bowl with a clean shower cap or your choice of cover and leave the bowl on the counter for 2 hours.

Step 2: After the 2 hours, perform the first set of pulls and folds on the dough. During this first set of pulls and folds the dough will still be sticky but keep working with it. The butter will still not be fully mixed in yet. Cover the bowl again and leave it to sit on the counter.

Step 3: After another hour, perform another set of pulls and folds on the dough, covering the bowl afterward. The dough will remain sticky but nicely stretchy and will come together into a soft ball. Cover the bowl again.

Step 4: Leave the covered bowl on the counter overnight, typically 8 to 12 hours, at 64 to 68°F (18 to 20°C).

Step 5: In the morning, hopefully the dough will have grown to double in size. If the dough has not doubled yet, allow it a few more hours to continue to proof. Once it has doubled in size, place the bowl of untouched dough in the fridge for at least an hour. This will make it easier to handle.

After this time, turn the dough out onto a floured surface. Using your fingers, push and stretch the dough into a rectangle 18 inches (45 cm) long and 12 inches (30 cm) wide. Sprinkle the frozen raspberries, chocolate chips and honeycomb pieces evenly all over the dough, then roll one long side toward the other, pulling the dough into a fat sausage. Cut the roll of dough into twelve equal pieces and place the cut sides up in the pan, tucking them in together. Cover the pan with its lid.

Top Tip: If you cannot find honeycomb pieces, use more dark chocolate chips for a total of 100 grams (⅔ cup), or a mix of dark and white chocolate chips.

Allow the dough to proof again for 1 hour at room temperature.

Step 6: When you are ready to bake, decide whether you would like to bake in a preheated oven or from a cold start. If preheating, set the oven to 400°F (200°C) convection or 425°F (220°C) conventional.

Step 7: If you preheated the oven, bake the rolls, covered, for 25 minutes. If you are using a cold start, place the covered pan of dough in the oven, set the temperature as above and set a timer for 30 minutes.

After this time, remove the lid and bake it uncovered for a further 10 minutes.

Step 8: Take the pan from the oven, carefully remove the round of rolls, remove the paper and sit them on a rack to allow them to cool briefly before serving. They are best eaten freshly baked.

Braided Milk Loaf

Playing with dough to make different shapes and looks is always fun, and serving a braided loaf always looks impressive. However, braiding sourdough can be challenging as the dough can be so soft and fluid. In this recipe, I have therefore replaced the water with milk to produce a firm dough that will be more manageable and satisfying to handle and braid. If the design looks overwhelming for a first attempt, I recommend doing a standard three-strand braid, and then the next time you can cut the dough into more pieces and make more intricate designs.

Equipment: I use my 10-inch (26-cm)-diameter enamel roaster pan; you can use your roaster, Dutch oven or a large, round, covered pan of a similar size. Line your choice with good-quality parchment paper.

Makes 1 standard loaf

50 g (¼ cup) active starter

325 g (1⅓ cups) milk, cold or at room temperature (I use reduced-fat or 2% milk, but you can also use full-fat/whole milk)

30 g (2 tbsp) oil (I use rapeseed oil)

500 g (4 cups) strong white bread flour

7 g (1 tsp) salt, or to taste

1 large egg, for glaze

Sesame or poppy seeds, to sprinkle over before baking (optional)

Step 1: In the early evening, in a large mixing bowl, roughly mix together all the ingredients, except the egg and optional seeds, until you have a shaggy, rough dough. Cover the bowl with a clean shower cap or your choice of cover and leave the bowl on the counter for 2 hours.

Step 2: After the 2 hours, perform the first set of pulls and folds until the dough comes together into a firm ball. This will be a smooth, stiff dough, but it will also be stretchy. Cover the bowl again and leave it on your counter.

Step 3: After another hour, do two more sets of pulls and folds on the dough, then cover it again. The dough will remain stiff but can be stretched.

Step 4: Leave the covered bowl on the counter overnight, typically 8 to 10 hours, at 64 to 68°F (18 to 20°C).

Step 5: The next morning, the dough will have doubled in size, have a smooth surface, and will be ready to make your braided loaf. Sprinkle a light layer of flour onto your kitchen counter and turn the dough out onto it. Cut the dough evenly into four pieces and hand-roll each piece out to an 18-inch (45-cm) strand. Sit the four pieces in a straight hashtag design on the counter, with 1-inch (2.5-cm) gaps, and each strand alternating over and under one another.

To braid, take each strand on the left and cross it over the strand to its right all the way around. Next, do the same going back the other way, around the whole set again. Repeat this going back the other way, left strands over right, then back the opposite way, right strands over left. By this point the dough will be coming together in a round design and the ends of the strands sticking out of the dough will now be very short. Pinch them together and tuck them underneath the dough.

Carefully lift the braided dough directly into your lined pan, place the lid on and leave it to proof again at room temperature until it has doubled in size. This may take 1 to 3 hours depending on your room temperature; the key here is to watch the dough. If it helps, take a photo before leaving it to proof as a reference so that you can compare the dough and judge the growth.

Step 6: When you are ready to bake, decide whether you would like to bake in a preheated oven or from a cold start. If preheating, set the oven to 350°F (180°C) convection or 400°F (200°C) conventional. Place your lined pan with the dough close by.

Whisk the egg and brush it all over the dough. Sprinkle it with seeds if you would like.

Step 7: If you preheated the oven, place the lid on the pan and bake it for 40 minutes. If you are using a cold start, place the covered pan of dough in the oven, set the temperature as above and set a timer for 45 minutes. If after this time the loaf looks pale, return the pan with the loaf back to the oven without the lid for 5 to 10 minutes until the loaf becomes a golden brown.

Step 8: Remove it from the oven and place the loaf onto a rack briefly to cool. Serve it when you are ready to eat.

The Loaf Tin
COLLECTIONS

Stress-Free Sandwich Loaf Sourdough Baking

The beauty of making and baking sandwich loaves is that you get perfectly shaped bread for sandwiches and toast, all with the benefit of the loaf tin holding the dough in place. This method, therefore, is perfect for those who struggle with shaping free-form loaves or when you want to be more experimental with doughs that can otherwise be difficult to shape.

In this section, I use a standard 900-gram (2-lb) loaf tin as well as a Pullman tin. I use the different tins to create bakes of slightly different sizes and shapes. For example, open Pullman tins produce taller, thinner loaves, but they are all interchangeable and can also be baked in a glass loaf pan.

Top Tip: I use silicone paper loaf tin liners or good-quality parchment paper to line my tins. If you do use a loaf tin liner to bake your loaf, remove it as soon as the loaf is baked and before placing it onto the rack to cool.

When baking in an unlined tin, spray a light layer of neutral oil, like rapeseed oil or vegetable oil, inside the tin to stop the loaf from sticking. If you find that the loaf does not easily fall out of the tin once it is baked, let it sit on the rack in the tin for 5 to 10 minutes and then try again. The steam will loosen the loaf and it will come out of the pan. Sit the baked loaf on the rack uncovered and if the steam softened the sides and base, they will crisp up again.

If you own two loaf tins, place the empty one upside down over the top of your tin with the dough in it for the first 30 minutes of the bake to boost growth and prevent the top of the loaf from browning too soon. Then carefully remove the top pan and continue to bake it uncovered.

Simplest Sandwich Loaves

This collection of sandwich loaves is designed to bring you a variety of easy-to-make doughs, which produce easy-to-slice loaves that are ideal for making sandwiches and are always a perfect fit for the toaster. The doughs do not need multiple handlings and the tins provide built-in shaping—simplicity rules!

Soft Everyday Sandwich Loaf

A wonderfully soft sandwich loaf is a treasure in any kitchen, whether eaten fresh with a slather of butter or used to make sandwiches or toast. This loaf is made using a mixture of strong white bread flour and a softer flour to produce soft slices with the added tang of sourdough in the background. If you use the white spelt flour option, the loaf will have an extra chewiness from the spelt that is really enjoyable.

Equipment: A Pullman loaf pan, external size 8½ x 5 x 4½ inches (21.5 x 12.5 x 11.5 cm), lined with parchment paper or lightly sprayed with a neutral or flavorless oil (see tips on page 43).

Makes 1 standard loaf

50 g (¼ cup) active starter

350 g (1½ cups) water

250 g (2 cups) strong white bread flour

250 g (2 cups) white spelt flour or all-purpose flour

7 g (1 tsp) salt, or to taste

Step 1: In the early evening, in a large mixing bowl, roughly mix together all the ingredients until you have a shaggy, sticky dough with no bits of dry flour. Cover the bowl with a clean shower cap or your choice of cover and leave the bowl on the counter for 2 hours.

Step 2: After the rest time, perform the first set of pulls and folds, lifting and stretching portions of the dough up and over the bowl, turning the bowl continuously to perform them evenly around the whole dough. Stop when the dough comes into a soft ball. The dough will be stretchy and easy to work with at this point, and will come into an easy, soft ball that will only hold its shape briefly before it starts to loosen up again. Cover the bowl again and leave it on your counter.

Step 3: After 1 more hour, do another set of pulls and folds on the dough; it will be stretchier now and will easily come into a ball. Cover the bowl again.

Step 4: Leave the covered bowl on the counter overnight, typically 8 to 10 hours, at 64 to 68°F (18 to 20°C).

(continued)

Soft Everyday Sandwich Loaf (Continued)

Step 5: In the morning, the dough will have grown to double, maybe even triple, in size, with a smooth, slightly domed surface. Have your loaf pan ready and place the paper liner on the counter. Gently lift and fold small handfuls of dough from one side of the bowl into the middle in a line, using the same pulling and folding action as used previously. Turn the bowl 180 degrees and do the same on the other side so that you have a thick sausage of dough in the middle of the bowl.

With a wetted hand, place your entire hand over the dough, turn the bowl upside down and gently ease the dough from the bowl into your hand. Place the dough, seam side down, on the paper and slip your hand out from underneath the dough. Use the paper to lift the dough into the pan, cover it with the same shower cap and leave it on the counter. Do not worry about creating a perfect shape with the dough; it will fill the pan and regain its shape during the final proof.

Allow the dough to proof again, letting it grow level with the edge of the pan until it is just peeking over the top. This may take 2 to 3 hours, depending on the temperature of your kitchen. The surface will become smooth and the dough will spread to fill the pan.

This step can also be done in the fridge for a longer, slower second proof—up to 24 hours—and can then be baked directly from the fridge.

Step 6: When you are ready to bake, decide whether you would like to bake in a preheated oven or from a cold start. If preheating, set the oven to 350°F (180°C) convection or 400°F (200°C) conventional.

Step 7: If you preheated the oven, put the lid on the pan and bake it for 45 minutes. If you are using a cold start, place the covered pan of dough in the oven, set the temperature as above and set a timer for 50 minutes.

Step 8: Remove the bread from the oven and the pan, tap the base of the loaf and if it sounds hollow, the loaf is baked. If not, return it to the oven, out of the pan, directly onto the rack to bake it for a further 5 to 10 minutes. Remove it from the oven and allow it to cool on a wire rack for at least an hour before slicing.

Top Tip: If you cannot find white spelt flour, use light spelt flour or whole-grain/whole wheat spelt flour.

Multi-Seed Sandwich Loaf

Sourdough loves seeds and I love seeds in sourdough. Doughs always respond well to having seeds in them, growing beautifully as they proof, while producing a firm dough that is a joy to handle. This baked loaf is studded with seeds in every tasty slice. I create my own seed mix, but you can use a premade mix or use a single type if you prefer.

Equipment: A 2-pound (900-g) loaf pan (9 x 5 inches [23 x 14 cm]), lined with parchment paper or lightly sprayed with a neutral or flavorless oil (see tips on page 43).

Makes 1 standard loaf

50 g (¼ cup) active starter

375 g (1¾ cups) water

500 g (4 cups) strong white bread flour

25 g (⅛ cup) golden flaxseeds

25 g (⅛ cup) poppy seeds

25 g (⅛ cup) millet seeds

25 g (⅛ cup) sunflower seeds

25 g (⅛ cup) pumpkin seeds

7 g (1 tsp) salt, or to taste

Step 1: In the early evening, in a large mixing bowl, roughly mix together all the ingredients until you have a shaggy, sticky dough with no bits of dry flour. Cover the bowl with a clean shower cap or your choice of cover and leave the bowl on the counter for 2 hours.

Step 2: After 2 hours, perform the first set of pulls and folds, lifting and pulling the dough up and over itself in the bowl; the dough will be stiff from the seeds but easy to stretch. Stop when it comes into a soft ball. Cover the bowl again and leave it on your counter for 1 more hour.

Step 3: After the hour, do another set of pulls and folds. The dough will be stretchier but still stiff and will easily come into a ball. Cover the bowl again.

Step 4: Leave the covered bowl on the counter overnight, typically 8 to 10 hours, at 64 to 68°F (18 to 20°C).

Step 5: In the morning, the dough will have grown to double in size. Have your pan ready and place the paper liner on the counter. Gently lift and fold small handfuls of dough from one side of the bowl into the middle in a line, using the same pulling and folding action as used previously. Turn the bowl 180 degrees and do the same on the other side so that you have a thick sausage of dough in the middle of the bowl.

With a wetted hand, place your whole hand over the dough, turn the bowl upside down and gently ease the dough from the bowl into your hand. Place the dough, seam side down, on the paper and slip your hand out from underneath the dough. Use the paper to lift the dough into the pan, cover it with the same shower cap and leave it on the counter.

Allow the dough to proof again, letting it grow level with the edge of the pan. This may take 2 to 3 hours, depending on the temperature of your kitchen. The surface will become smooth and the dough will spread to fill the pan. This step can also be done in the fridge for a longer, slower second proof—up to 24 hours—and can then be baked directly from the fridge.

Top Tips: You can follow my seed mix or create your own; you will need 125 g (½ cup plus 2 tbsp) of seeds in total.

This loaf can also be made using the same process as the Easy Shape Crusty White Loaf on page 15, using a round or oval banneton and baked in your bread pan.

Step 6: When you are ready to bake, decide whether you would like to bake in a preheated oven or from a cold start. If preheating, set the oven to 350°F (180°C) convection or 400°F (200°C) conventional.

Step 7: If you preheated the oven, put the lid on the pan and bake it for 45 minutes. If you are using a cold start, place the covered pan of dough in the oven, set the temperature as above and set a timer for 50 minutes.

Step 8: Remove the bread from the oven and the pan, tap the base of the loaf and if it sounds hollow, the loaf is baked. If not, return it to the oven, out of the pan, directly onto the rack to bake it for a further 5 to 10 minutes. Remove it from the oven and allow it to cool on a wire rack for at least an hour before slicing.

Same-Day Sandwich Loaf

This recipe enables you to make and eat a sourdough sandwich loaf all within one day. The use of extra starter teamed with a warm environment reduces the proofing time for those days when you wake up and decide that you would like to have freshly baked sourdough that same evening either for dinner or for breakfast or lunch the next day.

Equipment: A Pullman loaf pan, external size 8½ x 5 x 4½ inches (21.5 x 12.5 x 11.5 cm), lined with parchment paper or lightly sprayed with a neutral or flavorless oil (see tips on page 43).

Location: Use a warm place to proof the dough. I use my oven with the pilot light on and the door propped open, which creates an even temperature of 77°F (25°C). Alternatively, use a proofing box.

Makes 1 standard loaf

100 g (½ cup) active starter

350 g (1½ cups) warm water, around 100°F (38°C)

500 g (4 cups) strong white bread flour

7 g (1 tsp) salt, or to taste

Step 1: In the morning, in a medium-sized mixing bowl, roughly mix together all the ingredients until you have a shaggy, rough dough. Cover the bowl with a clean shower cap or your choice of cover and leave the bowl in your chosen warm spot. The dough will be sticky.

Step 2: After half an hour, perform the first set of pulls and folds until the dough feels less sticky and comes together into a soft ball. This will be a warm, soft, stretchy dough. Cover the bowl again and place it back in the warmth for half an hour.

Step 3: After the half an hour, perform another set of pulls and folds, repeating the same actions again; the dough should be nice and stretchy and bouncy, and it will come together into a smooth, soft ball. Place the covered bowl back in the warmth.

Step 4: Leave the dough in the warmth for approximately 3 hours, or until the dough has doubled in size.

Step 5: Once the dough is double its original size—it may be soft from the warm proofing, but it should not be floppy—have your pan ready and place the paper liner on the counter. Gently lift and fold small handfuls of dough from one side of the bowl into the middle in a line, using the same pulling and folding action as used previously. Turn the bowl 180 degrees and do the same on the other side so that you have a thick sausage of dough in the middle of the bowl.

With a wetted hand, place your whole hand over the dough, turn the bowl upside down and gently ease the dough from the bowl into your hand. Place the dough, seam side down, on the paper and slip your hand out from underneath the dough. Use the paper to lift the dough into the pan, cover it with the same shower cap and leave it on the counter.

Allow the dough to proof again, letting it grow level with the edge of the pan until it is just peeking over the top. This may take 2 to 3 hours, depending on the temperature of your kitchen. The surface will become smooth and the dough will spread to fill the pan.

Step 6: When you are ready to bake, decide whether you would like to bake in a preheated oven or from a cold start. If preheating, set the oven to 350°F (180°C) convection or 400°F (200°C) conventional.

Step 7: If you preheated the oven, bake it for 45 minutes. If you are using a cold start, place the pan of dough in the oven, set the temperature as above and set a timer for 50 minutes.

Step 8: Remove the loaf from the oven and the pan, tap the base of the loaf and if it sounds hollow, the loaf is baked. If not, return it to the oven, out of the pan, directly onto the rack to bake it for a further 5 to 10 minutes. Remove it from the oven and allow it to cool on a wire rack for at least an hour before slicing.

Whey and Honey Sandwich Loaf

Whey is the liquid left over from making cheese or yogurt, or from draining yogurt to make it thicker or to make labneh. Adding whey to a dough means that what would otherwise be considered a by-product and thrown away can be put to good use, plus it adds a wonderful aroma to the bread and a softness to the baked loaf. With the addition of the honey, this loaf is almost brioche-like in its flavor and texture.

Equipment: A Pullman loaf pan, external size 8½ x 5 x 4½ inches (21.5 x 12.5 x 11.5 cm), lined with parchment paper or lightly sprayed with a neutral or flavorless oil (see tips on page 43).

Makes 1 standard loaf

50 g (¼ cup) active starter

450 g (2 cups) whey

600 g (4½ cups) strong white bread flour

50 g (¼ cup) runny honey

7 g (1 tsp) salt, or to taste

Step 1: In the early evening, in a large mixing bowl, roughly mix together all the ingredients until you have a shaggy, rough dough. Cover the bowl with a clean shower cap or your choice of cover and leave the bowl on the counter for 2 hours.

Step 2: After 2 hours, perform the first set of pulls and folds until the dough feels less sticky and comes together into a soft ball. The dough will be wonderfully stretchy and will come into a bouncy, smooth ball. It will not hold its shape for long, which is fine. Cover the bowl again and leave it on your counter.

Step 3: After an hour, do one more set of pulls and folds on the dough, covering the dough again afterward. The dough will be stretchy and silky.

Step 4: Leave the covered bowl on the counter overnight, typically 8 to 10 hours, at 64 to 68°F (18 to 20°C).

Step 5: In the morning, the dough will have grown to double, possibly almost triple, in size. This will be a smooth dough, easy to handle and work with. Gently but firmly perform a final set of pulls and folds on the dough to pull it into a ball and pick it up.

Place the dough, smooth side up, into the prepared pan. Cover the pan with the same shower cap and place it on the counter to proof again until the dough is level with the top edges of the pan; this may take several hours depending on the temperature in your kitchen. The key is to watch the dough and to allow it time to do this important step. As a guide, this can take anywhere from 4 to 6 hours in my kitchen.

This step can also be done in the fridge for a longer, slower second proof—up to 24 hours—and can then be baked directly from the fridge.

Top Tip: If you do not have access to whey, mix 50 grams (¼ cup) of plain/natural yogurt with 400 grams (1¾ cups) of water and stir them well before adding it to the dough mix.

Step 6: When you are ready to bake, decide whether you would like to bake in a preheated oven or from a cold start. If preheating, set the oven to 350°F (180°C) convection or 400°F (200°C) conventional.

Step 7: If you preheated the oven, bake it for 45 minutes. If you are using a cold start, place the covered pan of dough in the oven, set the temperature as directed and set a timer for 50 minutes.

Step 8: Once it is baked, remove from the pan and tap the base of the loaf. If it sounds hollow, the loaf is baked. If not, return it to the oven, out of the pan, directly onto the rack to bake for a further 5 to 10 minutes. Remove it from the oven and allow it to cool on a wire rack for at least an hour before slicing.

Same-Day Perfectly Square Soft Sandwich Loaf

Pullman loaf pans produce an all-over square-edged loaf perfect for sandwiches and toast. This version is made with the addition of potato flakes in the dough, which add a softness to the baked loaf. If you do not have potato flakes, milk powder works perfectly instead. This recipe was designed to be made in one day, but the dough can be refrigerated overnight and baked the following morning if life gets in the way.

Equipment: A Pullman loaf pan, external size 8½ x 5 x 4½ inches (21.5 x 12.5 x 11.5 cm), lined with parchment paper or lightly sprayed with a neutral or flavorless oil (see tips on page 43).

Location: Use a warm place to proof the dough. I use my oven with the pilot light on and the door propped open, which creates an even temperature of 77°F (25°C). Alternatively, use a proofing box.

Makes 1 standard loaf

100 g (½ cup) active starter

350 g (1½ cups) warm water, around 100°F (38°C)

425 g (3½ cups) strong white bread flour

25 g (¼ cup) dried potato flakes or milk powder

7 g (1 tsp) salt, or to taste

Step 1: In a medium-sized mixing bowl, roughly mix together all the ingredients until you have a shaggy, rough dough. The dough will be sticky. Cover the bowl with a clean shower cap or your choice of cover and leave the bowl in your chosen warm spot.

Step 2: After half an hour, perform the first set of pulls and folds until the dough feels less sticky and comes together into a soft ball. This will be a warm, soft, stretchy dough. Cover the bowl again and place it back in the warmth.

Step 3: After half an hour, perform the next set of pulls and folds; the dough should be nice and stretchy and bouncy, and it will come together into a smooth, soft ball. Place the covered bowl back in the warmth for another 30 minutes.

Step 4: Perform the last set of pulls and folds; the dough should come together into a nice, smooth, bouncy ball. Place the covered bowl back in the warmth for the next 3 hours, or until the dough has doubled in size.

Step 5: Once the dough is double its original size—it may be soft from the warm proofing, but it should not be floppy—gently but firmly perform a set of pulls and folds on the dough to pull it into a ball. Place the dough, smooth side down, into your prepared pan. Cover the pan with the same cover and place it back in your warm place until the dough grows up to an inch (2.5 cm) below the top edges of the pan. This will take 1½ to 2 hours. This step can also be done in the fridge for a longer, slower second proof—up to 24 hours—and can then be baked directly from the fridge.

Step 6: When you are ready to bake, decide whether you would like to bake in a preheated oven or from a cold start. If preheating, set the oven to 350°F (180°C) convection or 400°F (200°C) conventional.

Step 7: If you preheated the oven, put the lid on the pan and bake it for 45 minutes. If you are using a cold start, place the covered pan of dough in the oven, set the temperature as above and set a timer for 50 minutes.

Step 8: Remove the loaf from the oven and the pan, tap the base of the loaf and if it sounds hollow, the loaf is baked. If not, return it to the oven, out of the pan, directly onto the rack to bake it for a further 5 to 10 minutes. Remove it from the oven and allow it to cool on a wire rack for at least an hour before slicing.

Super Square Whey Loaf

By replacing the water with whey in this loaf, the dough becomes silky and smooth, and the baked loaf is wonderfully sour and chewy. The added fat from the dairy means that the dough will bake to a deeper color, which also adds flavor to the loaf.

Equipment: A Pullman loaf pan, external size 8½ x 5 x 4½ inches (21.5 x 12.5 x 11.5 cm), lined with parchment paper or lightly sprayed with a neutral or flavorless oil (see tips on page 43).

Makes 1 standard loaf

50 g (¼ cup) active starter

350 g (1½ cups) whey

450 g (3¾ cups) strong white bread flour

7 g (1 tsp) salt, or to taste

Step 1: In the early evening, in a large mixing bowl, roughly mix together all the ingredients until you have a shaggy, sticky dough with no bits of dry flour. Cover the bowl with a clean shower cap or your choice of cover and leave the bowl on the counter for 2 hours.

Step 2: After 2 hours, perform the first set of pulls and folds; the dough will be soft and sticky but stretchy. Stop when it comes into a soft ball. Cover the bowl again and leave it on your counter for 1 more hour.

Step 3: After the hour, do another set of pulls and folds on the dough. It will be even stretchier now and will easily come into a bouncy ball. Cover the bowl again.

Step 4: Leave the covered bowl on the counter overnight, typically 8 to 10 hours, at 64 to 68°F (18 to 20°C).

Step 5: In the morning, the dough will have grown to double, possibly almost triple, in size. It will have an uneven textured surface.

Gently lift and fold small handfuls of dough from one side of the bowl into the middle in a line, using the same pulling and folding action as used previously. Turn the bowl 180 degrees and do the same on the other side so that you have a thick sausage of dough in the middle of the bowl. Knit and pinch the two sides together across the top.

Place your whole hand over the dough, turn the bowl upside down and gently ease the dough from the bowl into your hand. Place the dough, seam side down, into the prepared pan and slide your hand out. Cover the pan with the same shower cap and place it on the counter to proof again until the dough is level with the top edges of the pan. The key is to watch the dough and to allow it time to do this important step. As a guide, this can take anywhere from 4 to 6 hours in my kitchen depending on the temperature.

Step 6: When you are ready to bake, decide whether you would like to bake in a preheated oven or from a cold start. If preheating, set the oven to 350°F (180°C) convection or 400°F (200°C) conventional.

Step 7: If you preheated the oven, put the lid on the pan and bake it for 45 minutes. If you are using a cold start, place the covered pan of dough in the oven, set the temperature as above and set a timer for 50 minutes.

Step 8: Remove the bread from the oven and the pan, tap the base of the loaf and if it sounds hollow, the loaf is baked. If not, return it to the oven, out of the pan, directly onto the rack to bake it for a further 5 to 10 minutes. Remove it from the oven and allow it to cool on a wire rack for at least an hour before slicing.

Whole-Grain Spelt Square Loaf

Spelt flour is one of the tastiest flours I have ever used, whether it is the light, white or whole-grain version. When baking with it in a free-form loaf, it needs to be supported by some strong flour as the spelt flour will not hold its shape alone well. If I tried to bake this all-spelt dough as a free-form loaf, it would spread and bake to a flat disk. However, a loaf tin changes the game with spelt flour! In this recipe, we can use spelt flour on its own as the Pullman tin will provide the support the dough needs.

Equipment: A Pullman loaf pan, external size 8½ x 5 x 4½ inches (21.5 x 12.5 x 11.5 cm), lined with parchment paper or lightly sprayed with a neutral or flavorless oil (see tips on page 43).

Makes 1 standard loaf

50 g (¼ cup) active starter

350 g (1½ cups) water

450 g (3¾ cups) whole-grain spelt flour

7 g (1 tsp) salt, or to taste

Top Tip: This recipe will also work with light or white spelt flour and will result in an equally tasty but slightly lighter loaf.

Step 1: In the early evening, in a large mixing bowl, roughly mix together all the ingredients until you have a shaggy, sticky dough with no bits of dry flour. Cover the bowl with a clean shower cap or your choice of cover and leave the bowl on the counter for 2 hours.

Step 2: After 2 hours, perform the first set of pulls and folds; the dough will be stiff and spongy, and you may need to fold it over onto itself if it does not want to stretch yet. Stop when it comes into a ball that holds its shape. Cover the bowl again and leave it on your counter for 1 more hour.

Step 3: After the hour, do another set of pulls and folds on the dough; it will be stretchier now and will easily come into a ball. Cover the bowl again.

Step 4: Leave the covered bowl on the counter overnight, typically 8 to 10 hours, at 64 to 68°F (18 to 20°C).

Step 5: In the morning, the dough will have grown to double, possibly almost triple, in size. It will have an uneven textured surface. Gently lift and fold small handfuls of dough from one side of the bowl into the middle in a line, using the same pulling and folding action as used previously. Turn the bowl 180 degrees and do the same on the other side so that you have a thick sausage of dough in the middle of the bowl. Knit and pinch the two sides together across the top.

The dough will seem to collapse as you pull it together at this stage. This is normal, have no fear.

Place your whole hand over the dough, turn the bowl upside down and gently ease the dough from the bowl into your hand. Place the dough, seam side down, into the prepared pan and slide your hand out. Cover the pan with the same shower cap and place it on the counter to proof again until the dough is level with the top edges of the pan. The key is to watch the dough and to allow it time to do this important step. As a guide, this can take anywhere from 4 to 6 hours in my kitchen depending on the temperature.

Step 6: When you are ready to bake, decide whether you would like to bake in a preheated oven or from a cold start. If preheating, set the oven to 350°F (180°C) convection or 400°F (200°C) conventional.

Step 7: If you preheated the oven, put the lid on the pan and bake it for 45 minutes. If you are using a cold start, place the covered pan of dough in the oven, set the temperature as above and set a timer for 50 minutes.

Step 8: Remove the bread from the oven and the pan, tap the base of the loaf and if it sounds hollow, the loaf is baked. If not, return it to the oven, out of the pan, directly onto the rack to bake it for a further 5 to 10 minutes. Remove it from the oven and allow it to cool on a wire rack for at least an hour before slicing.

Same-Day White and Rye Loaf with Mixed Seeds

This recipe will give you a hearty rye loaf that is packed with seeds. Slice it thin and eat it Nordic-style, or slice it thicker and eat it Elaine-style. Just top it with butter or your own favorite topping for a filling, healthy, protein-packed breakfast, lunch, dinner or snack. This is a very simple loaf to make. The large portion of dark rye flour in the dough means that it is not a dough that can be stretched and pulled like other doughs, and in my tests, I have found that merely mixing the dough, letting it proof and then baking it works perfectly. So for this loaf, it is literally a case of mix it, proof it, bake it, done!

Equipment: A Pullman loaf pan, external size 8½ x 5 x 4½ inches (21.5 x 12.5 x 11.5 cm), lined with parchment paper or lightly sprayed with a neutral or flavorless oil (see tips on page 43).

Location: Use a warm place to proof the dough. I use my oven with the pilot light on and the door propped open, which creates an even temperature of 77°F (25°C). Alternatively, use a proofing box.

Makes 1 standard loaf

100 g (½ cup) active starter

300 g (1¼ cups) warm water, around 100°F (38°C)

150 g (1 cup) strong white bread flour

250 g (scant 2½ cups) dark rye flour

50 g (¼ cup) runny honey

50 g (⅓ cup) pumpkin seeds

50 g (⅓ cup) sunflower seeds

25 g (⅛ cup) flaxseeds

50 g (½ cup) rolled oats, rye flakes or wheat flakes

7 g (1 tsp) salt, or to taste

Step 1: In the morning, in a medium-sized mixing bowl, mix together all the ingredients. It will be a heavy, sticky dough. This dough is now ready to move into your lined tin. For ease, I use a tablespoon to literally "spoon" the mixture into my tin. Do not worry what it looks like in the tin; all you need to do is get all the dough into the tin. Cover the tin with a clean shower cap or your choice of cover and place it in your chosen warm spot.

Step 2: Leave the covered dough in your warm location for 8 hours, or until it reaches almost to the top of the pan.

Step 3: Once the dough has grown, decide whether you would like to bake in a preheated oven or from a cold start. If preheating, set the oven to 350°F (180°C) convection or 400°F (200°C) conventional.

If you preheated the oven, put the lid on the pan and bake it for 40 minutes. If you are using a cold start, place the covered pan of dough in the oven, set the temperature as above and set a timer for 45 minutes.

Step 4: Remove the loaf from the oven and the pan, remove the liner, tap the base of the loaf and if it sounds hollow, the loaf is baked. If not, return it to the oven, out of the pan, directly onto the rack to bake it for a further 5 to 10 minutes. Remove it from the oven and allow it to cool on a wire rack for at least 2 hours before slicing.

Top Tip: To develop a deeper flavor, follow the Simplest Ancient-Grain Loaf (page 63) steps.

Simplest Ancient-Grain Loaf

Ancient-grain flours, such as spelt, einkorn, emmer and rye flour can be hard to work with on their own. They cannot be stretched or worked with in the same way as modern flours, but they produce deep-flavored whole-grain loaves that taste so good I have developed this recipe to enable everyone to be able to make fully whole-grain, ancient-grain loaves as easily as possible. This recipe is truly simple: Just mix it, leave it, bake it and it will give you a weighty baked loaf bursting with flavor and whole-grain goodness.

Equipment: A Pullman loaf pan, external size 8½ x 5 x 4½ inches (21.5 x 12.5 x 11.5 cm), lined with parchment paper or lightly sprayed with a neutral or flavorless oil (see tips on page 43).

Makes 1 standard loaf

50 g (¼ cup) active starter

400 g (1¾ cups) water

400 g (3½ cups) ancient-grain flour of your choice (I use a mix of light spelt and dark rye flours; you can also use whole-grain einkorn flour, emmer flour or whole-grain spelt or rye flour on their own or mixed)

7 g (1 tsp) salt, or to taste

Top Tip: I use 70% light spelt flour and 30% dark rye flour. To recreate this mix, use 280 grams (2½ cups) of light spelt flour, and 120 grams (1 cup) of dark rye flour. If you cannot find light spelt flour, use all whole-grain or half white and half whole-grain spelt flour.

Step 1: In a medium-sized mixing bowl, mix together all the ingredients. It will be a heavy, sticky dough. Use a tablespoon to move the dough into your lined tin and cover it with a clean shower cap or your choice of cover.

The spelt and rye flour mix I use makes a spongy dough that can be pulled into a ball and placed into the tin. A dough made with solely einkorn, emmer or rye flours will need to be spooned into the tin. This dough does not need to be shaped in any way.

Step 2: Leave the covered dough on your kitchen counter until it reaches almost to the top of the pan. Mine took 18 hours at room temperatures between 18 and 20°C (64 to 68°F). This long proof allows the dough to grow slowly and develop a deep flavor at the same time.

Step 3: Once the dough has grown, decide whether you would like to bake in a preheated oven or from a cold start. If preheating, set the oven to 350°F (180°C) convection or 400°F (200°C) conventional.

If you preheated the oven, put the lid on the pan and bake it for 40 minutes. If you are using a cold start, place the covered pan of dough in the oven, set the temperature as above and set a timer for 45 minutes.

Step 4: Remove the loaf from the oven and the pan, remove the liner, tap the base of the loaf and if it sounds hollow, the loaf is baked. If not, return it to the oven, out of the pan, directly onto the rack to bake it for a further 5 to 10 minutes. Remove it from the oven and allow it to cool on a wire rack for at least 2 hours before slicing.

Top Tip: For a faster version, follow the steps in the Same-Day White and Rye Loaf with Mixed Seeds (page 60).

Flavored Sandwich Loaves

This collection of recipes is a flavor overload, taking my sourdough sandwich loaves to new heights with the addition of sweet and savory add-ins and fillings to provide bread for your table that tickles everyone's taste buds. In this section, you will find a Same-Day Cheese and Ketchup Babka (page 70) and a Fast Spelt, Dried Fruit, Nuts and Seeds Loaf (page 86), plus a loaf with chocolate and hazelnuts, one with roasted garlic and bulgur wheat, one with olive oil and spices and more, all in various mixes that I hope you will love.

Many of these loaves can also be made using the same process as the Easy Shape Crusty White Loaf on page 15, using a round or oval banneton and baked in your bread pan.

Peanut Butter and Jelly Babka

I must confess, this was my first-ever experience of "peanut butter and jelly," and oh my, I was hooked after my first taste. As I am in the U.K., we do not have jelly available as a standard product so I use a firm, seedless strawberry jam; you can use the jam of your choice or jelly. You can also use smooth or crunchy peanut butter. If you like peanut butter and jelly, you will love this filled babka!

Equipment: A 2-pound (900-g) loaf pan (9 x 5 inches [23 x 14 cm]), lined with parchment paper or sprayed lightly with a neutral or flavorless oil (see tips on page 43).

Makes 1 standard loaf

50 g (¼ cup) active starter

350 g (1½ cups) reduced-fat milk, cold or at room temperature (any type of dairy or plant-based milk works; I also like using oat milk in this dough)

500 g (4 cups) strong white bread flour

7 g (1 tsp) salt, or to taste

Filling

50 g (¼ cup) peanut butter (smooth or crunchy)

100 g (⅓ cup) jelly/jam of your choice

Step 1: In the early evening, in a medium-sized or large mixing bowl, roughly mix together all the ingredients, except the peanut butter and jam/jelly until you have a rough dough. Cover the bowl with a clean shower cap or your choice of cover and leave the bowl on the counter for 2 hours.

Step 2: After the 2-hour rest, perform the first set of pulls and folds. The dough will be stiff initially but will soon become smooth and come into a ball; at that point, stop. Cover the bowl again and leave it on your counter.

Step 3: After an hour, perform one more set of pulls and folds on the dough covering the dough again afterward. It will be stiff, slightly stretchier and smooth, and will quickly come into a firm ball.

Step 4: Leave the covered bowl on the counter overnight, typically 8 to 10 hours, at 64 to 68°F (18 to 20°C).

Step 5: The next morning, the dough will be doubled in size, with a smooth surface, typical of milk-based doughs. Place the dough, untouched but still covered, in the fridge for at least an hour until you are ready to use it. This dough can now be baked after an hour, or at any time during the day or evening—or the following morning. In the fridge, the dough will firm up, making it easier to work with later.

(continued)

Peanut Butter and Jelly Babka (Continued)

Step 6: After the time in the fridge, when you are ready, sprinkle flour over your kitchen counter and lay the pan liner open alongside the dough. Using a bowl scraper or your hands, gently ease the risen dough from the bowl onto the counter. Use your fingertips to start stretching and pushing out the dough until it becomes an 8 x 15¾–inch (20 x 40–cm) rectangle with an even thickness all over. This dough will be firm and easy to work with due to the milk in it. Stretch it out gently, being careful not to make holes in the dough.

Spread the peanut butter all over the dough, then spread a layer of jelly over the top. Roll up the dough from one of the shorter edges toward the other to make an even roll of dough. Once rolled, use a dough knife or sharp knife to cut the sausage lengthwise down the middle into two equal pieces. Twist the two pieces together, then lift the whole dough onto your paper liner and use the paper to lift it into your pan. Allow the dough to proof again, letting it grow level with the edge of the pan. This may take 2 to 4 hours, depending on the temperature of your kitchen.

This step can also be done in the fridge for a longer, slower second proof—up to 24 hours—and can then be baked directly from the fridge.

Once the dough has grown up to level with the edge of the pan, bake it.

Step 7: When you are ready to bake, decide whether you would like to bake in a preheated oven or from a cold start. If preheating, set the oven to 350°F (180°C) convection or 400°F (200°C) conventional.

Step 8: If you preheated the oven, bake it uncovered for 40 to 45 minutes. If you are using a cold start, place the uncovered pan of dough in the oven, set the temperature as above and set a timer for 45 to 50 minutes.

Step 9: Remove the loaf from the oven and the pan, remove the paper, tap the base of the loaf and if it sounds hollow, the loaf is baked. If not, return it to the oven, out of the pan, directly onto the oven rack to bake it for a further 5 to 10 minutes. Remove the loaf from the oven and allow it to cool briefly before slicing and tucking in!

Top Tip: If the jam/jelly starts to brown too much while the babka is baking, cover the tin with another tin the same size, or with foil, to prevent it from burning.

Dried Fruits and Seeds Loaf

I always have endless jars of dried fruits and seeds in my cupboards, and if I can stop myself from eating them for long enough, they are a perfect addition to a loaf of sourdough. This loaf is made with a seeded dough that is stretched and filled with a mix of dried fruits after the main overnight proof. This way the added ingredients are evenly mixed through the baked loaf and each slice is a dried fruit and seed lover's gift.

Equipment: A 2-pound (900-g) loaf pan (9 x 5 inches [23 x 14 cm]), lined with parchment paper or sprayed lightly with a neutral or flavorless oil (see tips on page 43).

Makes 1 standard loaf

50 g (¼ cup) active starter

375 g (1¾ cups) water

500 g (4 cups) strong white bread flour

50 g (⅓ cup) sunflower seeds

25 g (⅛ cup) flaxseeds

25 g (⅛ cup) chia seeds

7 g (1 tsp) salt, or to taste

Rice flour, for dusting the counter

Filling

5 soft dried figs, cut in half

10 soft, dried whole apricots

15 fat raisins

30 dried cranberries

Step 1: In the early evening, in a large mixing bowl, roughly mix together all the ingredients, including the seeds but except the fillings and rice flour, until you have a shaggy, rough dough. Cover the bowl with a clean shower cap or your choice of cover and leave the bowl on the counter for 2 hours.

Step 2: After 2 hours, perform the first set of pulls and folds until the dough feels less sticky and comes together into a firm, seed-speckled, heavy ball. Cover the bowl again and leave it on your counter.

Step 3: During the next few hours, do two more sets of pulls and folds on the dough, covering it after each set. This dough will be heavy and full of seeds. Perform the final set before going to bed.

Step 4: Leave the covered bowl on the counter overnight, typically 8 to 10 hours, at 64 to 68°F (18 to 20°C).

Step 5: In the morning, the dough will have grown to double in size, with a smooth surface textured with seeds. Sprinkle rice flour over your kitchen counter and lay the pan liner open alongside the dough. Using a bowl scraper or your hands, gently ease the risen dough from the bowl onto the counter. Use your fingertips to start stretching and pushing out the dough, until it becomes an 8 x 15¾–inch (20 x 40–cm) rectangle with an even thickness all over. The dough will want to pull back as you stretch it; continue to pull it gently, being careful not to make holes in the dough.

Sprinkle the dried fruits evenly over the stretched dough. Roll up the dough from one of the shorter edges toward the other to make an even roll of dough. Lift the sausage of dough and place it smooth side up on your paper liner. Using the liner, lift the dough into your waiting loaf pan, cover it with the same shower cap and place it on the counter to proof again. Once the dough has grown so that it is 1 inch (2.5 cm) over the edge of the pan, bake it.

This step can also be done in the fridge for a longer, slower second proof—up to 24 hours—and can then be baked directly from the fridge.

Step 6: When you are ready to bake, decide whether you would like to bake in a preheated oven or from a cold start. If preheating, set the oven to 350°F (180°C) convection or 400°F (200°C) conventional.

Step 7: If you preheated the oven, bake it uncovered for 40 to 45 minutes. If you are using a cold start, place the uncovered pan of dough in the oven, set the temperature as above and set a timer for 45 to 50 minutes.

Step 8: Remove the loaf from the oven and the pan, remove the liner, tap the base of the loaf and if it sounds hollow, the loaf is baked. If not, return it to the oven, out of the pan, directly onto the rack to bake it for a further 5 to 10 minutes. After this time, allow the baked loaf to cool on a wire rack for at least an hour before slicing.

Same-Day Cheese and Ketchup Babka

This loaf is a favorite with my chief taste taster, my son, Ben—it is a marriage of great bread with fillings he loves! Cheese and ketchup creates a popular, tasty filling, but if you prefer an alternative, the ketchup can be replaced with the sauce of your choice (ideally of a similar consistency to ketchup or thicker). Choose cheese that melts well and has a strong flavor for great results. I have made this loaf using my same-day timetable; it can also be made using my overnight proof process as used for my Easy Shape Crusty White Loaf (page 15) recipe if you prefer.

Equipment: A 2-pound (900-g) loaf pan (9 x 5 inches [23 x 14 cm]), with a liner or parchment paper (see chapter introduction regarding interchangeable tins).

Location: Use a warm place to proof the dough. I use my oven with the pilot light on and the door propped open, which creates an even temperature of 77°F (25°C). Alternatively, use a proofing box.

Makes 1 standard loaf

100 g (½ cup) active starter

325 g (1⅓ cups) warm water, around 100°F (38°C)

500 g (4 cups) strong white bread flour

7 g (1 tsp) salt, or to taste

Filling

200 g (1 cup) grated hard, flavorful cheese (I use a strong Cheddar or Red Leicester cheese, or you can try some Lincolnshire Poacher or aged Comté)

100 g (½ cup) ketchup or sauce of your choice

Step 1: In a medium-sized mixing bowl, roughly mix together all the ingredients, except the fillings, until you have a shaggy, rough dough. The dough will be sticky. Cover the bowl with a clean shower cap or your choice of cover and leave the bowl in your chosen warm spot.

Step 2: After half an hour, perform the first set of pulls and folds. Turn the bowl slightly and repeat this as many times as is necessary until the dough feels less sticky and comes together into a soft ball. This will be a warm, soft dough. Cover the bowl again and place it back in the warmth.

Step 3: After half an hour, perform the next set of pulls and folds, repeating the same actions again; the dough should be nice and stretchy and bouncy, and it should come together into a smooth, soft ball. Place the covered bowl back in the warmth.

Step 4: After another half an hour, perform the last set of pulls and folds; the dough should come together into a nice, smooth, bouncy ball. Place the covered bowl back in the warmth for the next 3 hours, or until the dough has doubled in size.

(continued)

Same-Day Cheese and Ketchup Babka (Continued)

Step 5: Once the dough has grown to double in size, with a smooth surface, place it in the fridge for 30 to 60 minutes to stop it growing any more and to firm up the dough and make it easier to handle. Sprinkle flour over your kitchen counter and lay the pan liner open alongside the dough. Using a bowl scraper or your hands, gently ease the risen dough from the bowl onto the counter. Use your fingertips to start stretching and pushing out the dough, until it becomes an 8 x 15¾-inch (20 x 40-cm) rectangle with an even thickness all over. The dough will want to pull back as you stretch it; continue to pull it gently, being careful not to make holes in the dough.

Spread the ketchup all over the dough, then evenly sprinkle the cheese over the top. Roll up the dough from one of the shorter edges toward the other to make an even roll of dough. Once rolled, use a dough knife or sharp knife to cut the sausage lengthwise down the middle into two equal pieces. Twist the two pieces together, then lift the whole dough onto your paper liner and use the paper to lift it into your pan.

Allow the dough to proof again, letting it grow level with the edge of the pan. This may take 2 to 4 hours, depending on the temperature of your kitchen. I prefer to do this step on my counter; however, if you would like to speed this up, place the tin with the braided dough back into your warm location for 1 to 2 hours. Once the dough grows to the edge of the pan, bake it.

Step 6: When you are ready to bake, decide whether you would like to bake in a preheated oven or from a cold start. If preheating, set the oven to 350°F (180°C) convection or 400°F (200°C) conventional.

Step 7: If you preheated the oven, bake it uncovered for 40 to 45 minutes. If you are using a cold start, place the uncovered pan of dough in the oven, set the temperature as above and set a timer for 45 to 50 minutes.

Step 8: Remove the loaf from the oven and the pan, remove the paper, tap the base of the loaf and if it sounds hollow, the loaf is baked. If not, return it to the oven, out of the pan, directly onto the oven rack to bake it for a further 5 to 10 minutes. Remove the loaf from the oven and allow it to cool briefly before slicing and tucking in!

Top Tip: This loaf is best eaten warm once baked. It also freezes and defrosts well, and can be sliced and used to make great sandwiches.

Same-Day Beer and Peanut Loaf

Beer and bread share a long history, back to a time when bakeries were located next to breweries because the yeast from beer-making formed the starting point for bread doughs. To marry them in a loaf is an almost obvious partnership. Add in peanuts and the marriage is complete! This loaf works well eaten as it is but you can also follow my steps for making it into crackers (page 75) to create easy snacks or dip scoops.

Equipment: A 2-pound (900-g) loaf pan (9 x 5 inches [23 x 14 cm]), lined with parchment paper or sprayed lightly with a neutral or flavorless oil (see tips on page 43).

Location: Use a warm place to proof the dough. I use my oven with the pilot light on and the door propped open, which creates an even temperature of 77°F (25°C). Alternatively, use a proofing box.

Makes 1 standard loaf

100 g (½ cup) active starter

330 g (11½ fl oz) beer, use a full-bodied beer for best results (I use Old Speckled Hen®)

450 g (3¾ cups) strong white bread flour

100 g (⅔ cup) peanuts (I use dry roasted peanuts)

7 g (1 tsp) salt (see Top Tip)

Step 1: In a medium-sized mixing bowl, roughly mix together all the ingredients until you have a shaggy, rough dough, lumpy from the peanuts and aromatic from the beer. Cover the bowl with a clean shower cap or your choice of cover and leave the bowl in your chosen warm spot.

Step 2: After half an hour, perform the first set of pulls and folds. Turn the bowl slightly and repeat this as many times as is necessary until the dough feels less sticky and comes together into a soft ball. This dough will be warm, soft, stretchy and easy to work with, even with the nuts in it. Cover the bowl again and place it back in the warmth.

Step 3: After half an hour, perform another set of pulls and folds, repeating the same actions again; the dough should be nice and stretchy, and it will come together into a nice, smooth, soft ball. Place the covered bowl back in the warmth.

Step 4: Leave the dough in the warmth for approximately 3 hours, or until the dough has doubled in size.

Step 5: Once the dough is double its original size—it may be soft from the warm proofing, but it will be silky and easy to handle—have your pan ready and place the paper liner on the counter. Gently lift and fold small handfuls of dough from one side of the bowl into the middle in a line, using the same pulling and folding action as used previously. Turn the bowl 180 degrees and do the same on the other side so that you have a thick sausage of dough in the middle of the bowl.

(continued)

Same-Day Beer and Peanut Loaf (Continued)

With a wetted hand, place your whole hand over the dough, turn the bowl upside down and gently ease the dough from the bowl into your hand. Place the dough, seam side down, on the paper and slip your hand out from underneath the dough. Use the paper to lift the dough into the pan, cover it with the same shower cap and leave it on the counter.

Allow the dough to proof again, letting it grow level with the edge of the pan until it is just peeking over the top. This may take 2 to 3 hours, depending on the temperature of your kitchen. The surface will become smooth and the dough will spread to fill the pan.

This step can also be done in the fridge for a longer, slower second proof—up to 24 hours—and can then be baked directly from the fridge.

Step 6: When you are ready to bake, decide whether you would like to bake in a preheated oven or from a cold start. If preheating, set the oven to 350°F (180°C) convection or 400°F (200°C) conventional.

Step 7: If you preheated the oven, bake the loaf for 45 minutes. If you are using a cold start, place the pan of dough in the oven, set the temperature as above and set a timer for 50 minutes.

Step 8: Remove the loaf from the oven and the pan, tap the base of the loaf and if it sounds hollow, the loaf is baked. If not, return it to the oven, out of the pan, directly onto the rack to bake it for a further 5 to 10 minutes. Remove it from the oven and allow it to cool on a wire rack for at least an hour before slicing.

To Make Bread Crackers

Set the oven to 400°F (200°C) convection or 425°F (220°C) conventional.

Decide how much of the loaf you wish to make into crackers, and slice very thin slices from the loaf, 1/16 inch thick. Cut each slice in half lengthwise. Lay all the pieces on a baking sheet lined with parchment paper and spray or brush them all with a light layer of rapeseed or olive oil or melted butter. Bake them for 10 minutes, or until they are browned and crunchy.

Cool them slightly before serving.

Top Tip: If you are using salted peanuts you may not need the extra salt in the dough. With dry roasted peanuts the loaf still benefits from added salt, too.

Cheese and Chili Flake Loaf

Cheese and bread is such a classic combination that brings this loaf alive with flavor as well as the joy of melted cheese. I have added a chili fix, too, which can be as mild or strong as you choose. I use Aleppo chili flakes, which are a medium heat. I recommend using a cheese with a strong flavor or a combination of your favorite cheeses. This ensures that the flavor does not get lost in the loaf. I love to use sharp Cheddar cheese in my loaves, which is what I used in the loaf in the photo.

Equipment: A 2-pound (900-g) loaf pan (9 x 5 inches [23 x 14 cm]) or an open Pullman pan (external size 8½ x 5 x 4½ inches [21.5 x 12.5 x 11.5 cm]), lined with parchment paper or sprayed lightly with a neutral or flavorless oil (see tips on page 43).

Makes 1 standard loaf

50 g (¼ cup) active starter

350 g (1½ cups) water

500 g (4 cups) strong white bread flour, plus more for dusting

7 g (1 tbsp) Aleppo chili flakes, or spice blend of your choice

7 g (1 tsp) salt, or to taste

Filling

100 g (¾ cup) strong hard cheese, grated (I use a colored strong Cheddar in my loaf, but I often also use a mature or farmhouse Cheddar, or strong Red Leicester)

Step 1: In the early evening, in a large mixing bowl, roughly mix together all the ingredients, except for the cheese, until you have a shaggy, rough dough. Cover the bowl with a clean shower cap or your choice of cover and leave the bowl on the counter for 2 hours.

Step 2: After the 2 hours, perform the first set of pulls and folds until the dough feels less sticky and comes together into a soft pink and red speckled ball. Cover the bowl again and leave it on your counter.

Step 3: After 1 more hour, do one more set of pulls and folds on the dough, covering the dough again afterward.

Step 4: Leave the covered bowl on the counter overnight, typically 8 to 10 hours, at 64 to 68°F (18 to 20°C).

Step 5: In the morning, the dough will have grown to double in size, with a smooth surface. Sprinkle flour over your kitchen counter and lay the pan liner open alongside the dough. Using a bowl scraper or your hands, gently ease the risen dough from the bowl onto the counter. Use your fingertips to start stretching and pushing out the dough, until it becomes an 8 x 15¾-inch (20 x 40–cm) rectangle with an even thickness all over. The dough will want to pull back as you stretch it; continue to pull it gently, being careful not to make holes in the dough. Sprinkle the cheese evenly over the stretched dough. Roll up the dough from one of the shorter edges toward the other to make an even roll of dough.

Lift the dough and place it, smooth side up, on your paper liner. Using the liner, lift the dough into your waiting loaf pan, cover it with the same shower cap and place it on the counter to proof again.

This step can also be done in the fridge for a longer, slower second proof—up to 24 hours—and can then be baked directly from the fridge.

Once the dough has grown up to level with the edge of the pan, bake it.

Step 6: When you are ready to bake, decide whether you would like to bake in a preheated oven or from a cold start. If preheating, set the oven to 350°F (180°C) convection or 400°F (200°C) conventional.

Step 7: If you preheated the oven, bake it uncovered for 40 to 45 minutes. If you are using a cold start, place the uncovered pan of dough in the oven, set the temperature as above and set a timer for 45 to 50 minutes.

Step 8: Remove the loaf from the oven and the pan, remove the paper, tap the base of the loaf and if it sounds hollow, the loaf is baked. If not, return it to the oven, out of the pan, directly onto the oven rack to bake it for a further 5 to 10 minutes. Remove the loaf from the oven and allow it to cool on a wire rack for at least an hour before slicing.

Same-Day Olive Oil, Roasted Cumin, Coriander and Caraway Loaf

This loaf brings together a trio of spices that I use often in cooking and produces a highly aromatic and flavorful loaf as a result. The addition of the olive oil makes the dough smooth and silky to work with, adds a softness to the baked loaf and also rounds out the flavors of the spiced bread. The recipe is designed to be able to start making the dough in the morning and have a baked loaf ready to eat in the evening.

Equipment: A Pullman loaf pan, external size 8½ x 5 x 4½ inches (21.5 x 12.5 x 11.5 cm), lined with parchment paper or lightly sprayed with a neutral or flavorless oil (see tips on page 43).

Location: Use a warm place to proof the dough. I use my oven with the pilot light on and the door propped open, which creates an even temperature of 77°F (25°C). Alternatively, use a proofing box.

Makes 1 standard loaf

100 g (½ cup) active starter

325 g (1⅓ cups) warm water, around 100°F (38°C)

500 g (4 cups) strong white bread flour

30 g (2 tbsp) olive oil

7 g (1 tbsp) ground roasted cumin powder

7 g (1 tbsp) ground roasted coriander seeds

7 g (1 tbsp) ground roasted caraway seeds

7 g (1 tsp) salt, or to taste

Step 1: In the morning, in a medium-sized mixing bowl, roughly mix together all the ingredients until you have a shaggy, rough dough. Cover the bowl with a clean shower cap or your choice of cover and place the bowl in your chosen warm spot.

Step 2: After half an hour, perform the first set of pulls and folds. Turn the bowl slightly and repeat this as many times as is necessary until the dough feels less sticky and comes together into a soft ball. This will be a warm, soft, stretchy and very aromatic dough. Cover the bowl again and place it back in the warmth.

Step 3: After half an hour, perform another set of pulls and folds, repeating the same actions again; the dough should be nice and stretchy, and it will come together into a nice, smooth, soft ball. Place the covered bowl back in the warmth.

Step 4: Leave the dough in the warmth for approximately 3 hours, or until the dough has doubled in size.

Step 5: Once the dough is double its original size—it may be soft from the warm proofing, but it will be silky and easy to handle—have your pan ready and place the paper liner on the counter. Gently lift and fold small handfuls of dough from one side of the bowl into the middle in a line, using the same pulling and folding action as used previously. Turn the bowl 180 degrees and do the same on the other side so that you have a thick sausage of dough in the middle of the bowl.

With a wetted hand, place your whole hand over the dough, turn the bowl upside down and gently ease the dough from the bowl into your hand. Place the dough, seam side down, on the paper and slip your hand out from underneath the dough. Use the paper to lift the dough into the pan, cover it with the same shower cap and leave it on the counter. Allow the dough to proof again, letting it grow level with the edge of the pan and just peek over the top. This may take 2 to 3 hours, depending on the temperature of your kitchen. The surface will become smooth and the dough will spread to fill the pan.

The dough will still be warm and may proof quickly as a result. If you would prefer to speed it up even more, place the dough in its tin back in your warm location.

Step 6: When you are ready to bake, decide whether you would like to bake in a preheated oven or from a cold start. If preheating, set the oven to 350°F (180°C) convection or 400°F (200°C) conventional.

Step 7: If you preheated the oven, bake the loaf for 45 minutes. If you are using a cold start, place the pan of dough in the oven, set the temperature as above and set a timer for 50 minutes.

Step 8: Remove the loaf from the oven and the pan, tap the base of the loaf and if it sounds hollow, the loaf is baked. If not, return it to the oven, out of the pan, directly onto the rack to bake it for a further 5 to 10 minutes. Remove it from the oven and allow it to cool on a wire rack for at least an hour before slicing.

Dark Chocolate Chip, Hazelnut and Rye Loaf

Dark chocolate and hazelnut is a classic, delicious combination. Add in rye flour for a touch of whole grain sweetness plus your sourdough starter and you get a loaf bursting with flavor and all the goodness that a long sourdough proof brings to bread making.

Equipment: A Pullman loaf pan, external size 8½ x 5 x 4½ inches (21.5 x 12.5 x 11.5 cm), lined with parchment paper or lightly sprayed with a neutral or flavorless oil (see tips on page 43).

Makes 1 standard loaf

50 g (¼ cup) active starter

350 g (1½ cups) water

450 g (3¾ cups) strong white bread flour

50 g (¼ cup) dark rye flour

50 g (½ cup) chopped hazelnuts

100 g (½ cup) dark chocolate chips

7 g (1 tsp) salt, or to taste

Step 1: In the early evening, in a large mixing bowl, roughly mix together all the ingredients until you have a shaggy, rough dough. Cover the bowl with a clean shower cap or your choice of cover and leave the bowl on the counter for 2 hours.

Step 2: After 2 hours, perform the first set of pulls and folds until the dough feels less sticky and comes together into a soft chocolate and nut-studded ball. Cover the bowl again and leave it on your counter.

Step 3: After another hour of rest, do one more set of pulls and folds on the dough, covering the dough again afterward.

Step 4: Leave the covered bowl on the counter overnight, typically 8 to 10 hours, at 64 to 68°F (18 to 20°C).

Step 5: In the morning, the dough will have grown to double in size, with a smooth-ish surface. Have your pan ready and place the paper liner on the counter. Gently lift and fold small handfuls of dough from one side of the bowl into the middle in a line, using the same pulling and folding action as used previously. Turn the bowl 180 degrees and do the same on the other side so that you have a thick sausage of dough in the middle of the bowl.

With a wetted hand, place your whole hand over the dough, turn the bowl upside down and gently ease the dough from the bowl into your hand. Place the dough, seam side down, on the paper and slip your hand out from underneath the dough. Use the paper to lift the dough into the pan, cover it with the same shower cap and leave it on the counter. Allow the dough to proof again, letting it grow level with the edge of the pan until it is just peeking over the top. This may take 2 to 3 hours, depending on the temperature of your kitchen. The surface will become smooth and the dough will spread to fill the pan.

This step can also be done in the fridge for a longer, slower second proof—up to 24 hours—and can be baked directly from the fridge.

Top Tip: For a sweeter loaf, add 50 grams (¼ cup) of runny honey to the dough.

Step 6: When you are ready to bake, decide whether you would like to bake in a preheated oven or from a cold start. If preheating, set the oven to 350°F (180°C) convection or 400°F (200°C) conventional.

Step 7: If you preheated the oven, bake the loaf for 45 minutes. If you are using a cold start, place the pan of dough in the oven, set the temperature as above and set a timer for 50 minutes.

Step 8: Remove the loaf from the oven and the pan, tap the base of the loaf and if it sounds hollow, the loaf is baked. If not, return it to the oven, out of the pan, directly onto the rack to bake it for a further 5 to 10 minutes. Remove it from the oven and allow it to cool on a wire rack for at least an hour before slicing.

Bulgur Wheat, Roasted Garlic and Chili Oil Loaf

This aromatic loaf is wonderfully soft from the bulgur wheat and chili oil. On eating, the first experience of the loaf will be a soft, slightly moist texture, followed by bursts of garlic. The chili oil I use is quite strong and adds a chili kick that then comes through in the flavor. It is perfect eaten unadorned, dipped in more oil or as an accompaniment to a meal or dips.

Equipment: A Pullman loaf pan, external size 8½ x 5 x 4½ inches (21.5 x 12.5 x 11.5 cm), lined with parchment paper or lightly sprayed with a neutral or flavorless oil (see tips on page 43).

Makes 1 standard loaf

50 g (¼ cup) active starter

320 g (1¼ cups) water

450 g (3¾ cups) strong white bread flour

100 g (½ cup) cooked and cooled coarse bulgur wheat

50 g (¼ cup) roasted garlic

30 g (⅛ cup) chili oil

7 g (1 tsp) salt, or to taste

Step 1: In the early evening, in a medium-sized or large mixing bowl, roughly mix together all the ingredients until you have a sticky, rough dough. Cover the bowl with a clean shower cap or your choice of cover and leave the bowl on the counter for 2 hours.

Step 2: After the 2-hour rest, perform the first set of pulls and folds. The dough will be sticky, lumpy and textured with the grains, and it will come into a soft ball; at that point, stop. Cover the bowl again and leave it on your counter.

Step 3: After an hour, perform one more set of pulls and folds on the dough, covering the dough again afterward. It will be stretchier now but will remain sticky.

Step 4: Leave the covered bowl on the counter overnight, typically 8 to 10 hours, at 64 to 68°F (18 to 20°C).

Step 5: In the morning, the dough will have grown to double in size, with a smooth surface.

Have your pan ready and place the paper liner on the counter. Gently lift and fold small handfuls of dough from one side of the bowl into the middle in a line, using the same pulling and folding action used previously. Turn the bowl 180 degrees and do the same on the other side so that you have a thick sausage of dough in the middle of the bowl.

With a wetted hand, place your whole hand over the dough, turn the bowl upside down and gently ease the dough from the bowl into your hand. Place the dough, seam side down, on the paper and slip your hand out from underneath the dough. Use the paper to lift the dough into the pan, cover it with the same shower cap and leave it on the counter. Allow the dough to proof again, letting it grow level with the edge of the pan until it is just peeking over the top. This may take 2 to 3 hours, depending on the temperature of your kitchen. The surface will become smooth and the dough will spread to fill the pan.

Top Tip: To produce the amount of roasted garlic above, I roasted 4 small heads of garlic whole, then squeezed out the soft cloves once they had cooled.

This step can also be done in the fridge for a longer, slower second proof—up to 24 hours—and can then be baked directly from the fridge.

Step 6: When you are ready to bake, decide whether you would like to bake in a preheated oven or from a cold start. If preheating, set the oven to 350°F (180°C) convection or 400°F (200°C) conventional.

Step 7: If you preheated the oven, bake the loaf uncovered for 40 minutes. If you are using a cold start, place the uncovered pan of dough in the oven, set the temperature as above and set a timer for 45 minutes.

Step 8: Remove the loaf from the oven and the pan, remove the paper, tap the base of the loaf and if it sounds hollow, the loaf is baked. If not, return it to the oven, out of the pan, directly onto the rack to bake it for a further 5 to 10 minutes. Remove it from the oven and allow it to cool on a wire rack for at least an hour before slicing.

Satay-Swirled Black Sesame Seed Loaf

I happily find reasons to eat peanut butter in any form, so I love satay sauce. I make my own using chunky peanut butter to add an extra crunch. You can make your own or use store-bought satay sauce for this recipe. I enjoy this loaf on its own or eaten with a soup or steaming vegetable stew.

Equipment: A Pullman loaf pan, external size 8½ x 5 x 4½ inches (21.5 x 12.5 x 11.5 cm), lined with parchment paper or lightly sprayed with a neutral or flavorless oil (see tips on page 43).

Makes 1 standard loaf

50 g (¼ cup) active starter

350 g (1½ cups) water

500 g (4 cups) strong white bread flour, plus more for dusting

50 g (⅓ cup) black sesame seeds

7 g (1 tsp) salt, or to taste

Filling

200 g (1 cup) satay sauce, store-bought or homemade

Step 1: In the early evening, in a large mixing bowl, roughly mix together all the ingredients, except the satay sauce, until you have a shaggy, rough dough. Cover the bowl with a clean shower cap or your choice of cover and leave the bowl on the counter for 2 hours.

Step 2: After the 2 hours, perform the first set of pulls and folds until the dough feels less sticky and comes together into a soft ball speckled with black sesame seeds. Cover the bowl again and leave it on your counter.

Step 3: After another hour or so, do one more set of pulls and folds on the dough, which will be stretchy but slightly stiff from the seeds, covering the dough afterward.

Step 4: Leave the covered bowl on the counter overnight, typically 8 to 10 hours, at 64 to 68°F (18 to 20°C).

Step 5: In the morning, the dough will have grown to double in size, with a smooth surface. Sprinkle flour over your kitchen counter and lay the pan liner open alongside the dough. Using a bowl scraper or your hands, gently ease the risen dough from the bowl onto the counter. Use your fingertips to start stretching and pushing out the dough until it becomes an 8 x 15¾–inch (20 x 40–cm) rectangle with an even thickness all over. The dough will want to pull back as you stretch it; continue to pull it gently, being careful not to make holes in it.

Spread the satay sauce evenly over the stretched dough. Roll up the dough from one of the shorter edges toward the other to make an even roll of dough. Lift the sausage of dough and place it, smooth side up, into your loaf tin liner. Use the paper to lift the dough into the pan, cover it with the same shower cap and leave it on the counter.

Allow the dough to proof again, letting it grow level with the edge of the pan until it is just peeking over the top. This may take 2 to 3 hours, depending on the temperature of your kitchen. The surface will become smooth and the dough will spread to fill the pan.

Top Tips: If you do not have satay sauce, use peanut butter instead. Sprinkle chili flakes of your choice over the peanut butter to add the heat that satay sauce would bring.

This loaf can also be made using the same process as the Easy Shape Crusty White Loaf on page 15, using an oval banneton and baking it in your bread pan.

This step can also be done in the fridge for a longer, slower second proof—up to 24 hours long—and can then be baked directly from the fridge.

Step 6: When you are ready to bake, decide whether you would like to bake in a preheated oven or from a cold start. If preheating, set the oven to 350°F (180°C) convection or 400°F (200°C) conventional.

Step 7: If you preheated the oven, bake the loaf for 45 minutes. If you are using a cold start, place the pan of dough in the oven, set the temperature as above and set a timer for 50 minutes.

Step 8: Remove the loaf from the oven and the pan, tap the base of the loaf and if it sounds hollow, the loaf is baked. If not, return it to the oven, out of the pan, directly onto the rack to bake it for a further 5 to 10 minutes. Remove it from the oven and allow it to cool on a wire rack for at least an hour before slicing.

Fast Spelt, Dried Fruit, Nuts and Seeds Loaf

This loaf can be made and baked and eaten all within a couple of hours. With all of the added seeds, nuts and dried fruits, every single slice is a treat packed with flavor and texture, and it is very hard to stop eating! It is perfect eaten alone or slathered with butter, or with some blue cheese, which I love. The possibilities are endless. This is a heavy mix and produces a wholesome loaf.

Equipment: A Pullman loaf pan, external size 8½ x 5 x 4½ inches (21.5 x 12.5 x 11.5 cm), lined with parchment paper or lightly sprayed with a neutral or flavorless oil (see tips on page 43).

Makes 1 standard loaf

100 g (½ cup) starter (it can be recently fed, unfed, or discard)

400 g (1¾ cups) water

300 g (1¾ cups) all-purpose flour

200 g (1¼ cups) whole-grain spelt flour

100 g (1 cup) dried figs, cut in half

100 g (1 cup) dried apricots, cut in half

100 g (1 cup) walnuts

50 g (⅓ cup) dried cranberries

50 g (⅓ cup) raisins

50 g (⅓ cup) roasted pumpkin seeds

1 large egg

7 g (1 tsp) baking soda

4 g (½ tsp) baking powder

7 g (2 tsp) mixed spice (see Top Tips)

Step 1: In a medium-sized mixing bowl, combine all the ingredients. Mix them well to form a lumpy batter, ensuring no dry flour is left, but do not overmix.

Step 2: Spoon the mixture into your prepared loaf pan.

Step 3: When you are ready to bake, decide whether you would like to bake in a preheated oven or from a cold start. If preheating, set the oven to 350°F (180°C) for convection or 400°F (200°C) for conventional.

If you preheated the oven, bake the loaf uncovered for 50 to 60 minutes, or until a metal skewer or thin knife inserted into the center comes out clean. If you are using a cold start, place the uncovered pan of dough in the oven, set the temperature as above and set a timer for 60 minutes. Bake for the allotted time, or until a metal skewer or thin knife inserted into the center comes out clean.

Step 4: Remove the pan from the oven and place it on a rack with the loaf still inside. Allow it to sit for 10 to 15 minutes, then remove the loaf from the pan and liner. Serve it either warm or cooled.

For an egg-free option: Make a flax egg by mixing 7 grams (1 tbsp) of ground flaxseeds with 37 grams (2½ tbsp) of warm or room-temperature water. Stir, then allow it to sit for 5 minutes to thicken. Replace the egg with the flax egg.

Top Tips: The spice blend can be store-bought or homemade. Mine includes cinnamon, coriander, caraway, nutmeg, ginger and cloves. A pumpkin pie spice or apple pie spice mix would work equally well.

The amount of water I used was ideal with my flour and in my dough. If you feel that your dough could use more, then go for it. As this loaf is being baked in a tin, you do not need to be too worried about how it holds itself. This is not like a typical sourdough loaf; it is a heavy, fullsome loaf but tastes equally amazing!

The Cake Tin
COLLECTION

Creative Ways to Bake Baby Breads and Magnificent Flavor-Packed Loaves

How many cake tins do you have? I have quite a few and I never bake cakes! So, I use them for bread—a perfect solution. I also love using Bundt tins for my breads, partly because it is so unexpected and not what you would think of being able to bake sourdough in, and partly to create more uses for Bundt tins as they are often the most expensive pan that we own. These pans come in so many beautiful shapes and it means that our bread is not a "standard" loaf shape, but a pretty celebration of dough each time. These tins can also provide support for your dough, almost giving the dough walls to lean against, so if you struggle with your dough holding its shape, cake tins can take this worry out of your sourdough baking.

Round White Simple Baby Boule

This loaf is a scaled-down version of my standard loaf. This is a great size if you prefer smaller loaves or want to experiment with making loaves using different flours or new additions. For this loaf, I use a smaller banneton, which I have noted to the right. With smaller doughs, it is often easier to begin the process using a spatula or bowl scraper to do the first mix of the dough.

Equipment: A round banneton, 6¾ inches (17 cm) in diameter and 3¼ inches (8.5 cm) deep, or a cloth-lined bowl dusted with rice flour. Set aside an 8-inch (20-cm)-diameter cake tin with 3¾-inch (9.5-cm)-high sides, or a baking pan with a lid (or another cake tin or tin foil over the top), plus parchment paper or a cake tin liner.

Makes 1 small loaf

30 g (⅛ cup) active starter

200 g (¾ cup) water

300 g (2½ cups) strong white bread flour

4 g (½ tsp salt), or to taste

Rice flour, for dusting

Step 1: In the early evening, in a large mixing bowl, roughly mix together all the ingredients, except the rice flour, until you have a shaggy, rough dough. Cover the bowl with a clean shower cap or your choice of cover and leave the bowl on the counter for 2 hours.

Step 2: After this rest time, perform the first set of pulls and folds until the dough feels less sticky and comes together into a firm, smooth ball. Cover the bowl again and leave it on your counter.

Step 3: After 1 to 1½ hours, do another set of pulls and folds on the dough, covering the dough again afterward. Let it rest again for another hour, do one more set of pulls and folds, then cover the bowl again.

Step 4: Leave the covered bowl on the counter overnight, typically 8 to 10 hours, at 64 to 68°F (18 to 20°C).

Step 5: In the morning, you should be greeted by a bowl full of grown dough. Perform a set of pulls and folds to firmly pull the dough into a nice ball that holds its shape. Place your hand over the whole dough and lift it into the banneton, smooth side down. Sprinkle extra rice flour down the sides and over the top of the dough. Cover the banneton and place it in the fridge for 3 to 24 hours.

Step 6: When you are ready to bake, decide whether you would like to bake in a preheated oven or from a cold start. If preheating, set the oven to 425°F (220°C) convection or 450°F (230°C) conventional.

Remove the cover from the banneton, then place the parchment paper over the top of the banneton and put the pan upside down over the top of them both. With one hand under the banneton and one on the pan, turn it all over together to turn the dough out of the banneton and into the pan. Score the dome of dough.

Step 7: If you preheated the oven, put the lid on the pan or cover it with another cake tin or foil, and bake it for 40 minutes. If you are using a cold start, place the covered pan of dough in the oven, set the temperature as above and set a timer for 45 minutes. Remove the cover 10 minutes before the end of the baking time. After the full baking time, remove the pan from the oven. If you feel that it is looking pale, place the pan with the loaf back in the hot oven, minus the lid, for 5 to 10 minutes to brown the loaf to the color of your choice.

Step 8: Once it is baked, carefully remove the loaf from the pan, saving the parchment paper for next time, and allow the baked loaf to cool on a wire rack for at least an hour before slicing.

Same-Day Whole Wheat Baby Boule

This baby whole wheat loaf can be made, baked and eaten on the same day. This will be a denser and chewier loaf than all-white loaves and is packed full of flavor. With this dough, it is often easier to begin the process using a spatula or bowl scraper to perform the first mix of the dough as it is small and stiff.

Equipment: A round banneton, 6¾ inches (17 cm) in diameter and 3¼ inches (8.5 cm) deep, or a cloth-lined bowl, dusted with rice flour. Set aside an 8-inch (20-cm)-diameter cake tin with 3¾-inch (9.5-cm)-high sides, or a baking pan with a lid (or another cake tin or tin foil over the top), plus parchment paper or a cake tin liner.

Location: Use a warm place to proof the dough. I use my oven with the pilot light on and the door propped open, which creates an even temperature of 77°F (25°C). Alternatively, use a proofing box.

Makes 1 small loaf

60 g (¼ cup) active starter

250 g (1 cup) warm water, around 100°F (38°C)

300 g (2½ cups) whole wheat flour

4 g (½ tsp salt), or to taste

Rice flour, for dusting

Step 1: In the morning, using a medium-sized mixing bowl, roughly mix together all the ingredients, except the rice flour, until you have a shaggy, rough dough. The dough will be sticky. Cover the bowl with a clean shower cap or your choice of cover and leave the bowl in your chosen warm spot.

Step 2: After half an hour, perform the first set of pulls and folds. Turn the bowl slightly and repeat this as many times as is necessary until the dough feels less sticky and comes together into a soft ball. This will be a warm and soft dough, and will be slightly spongy, which is typical when using whole wheat flour. Cover the bowl again and place it back in the warmth.

Step 3: After half an hour, perform the next set of pulls and folds, repeating the same actions again; the dough should be warm and stretchy, and it should come together into an easy ball. Place the covered bowl back in the warmth.

Step 4: After another half an hour, perform the last set of pulls and folds; the dough should come together into a nice, smooth, bouncy ball. Place the covered bowl back in the warmth for the next 3 hours, or until the dough has doubled in size.

Step 5: Once the dough is double its original size—it may be soft from the warm proofing—perform pulls and folds on the dough to firmly form it into a nice smooth ball. Place your hand over the whole dough and lift it into the banneton, smooth side down. Sprinkle extra rice flour down the sides and over the top of the dough. Cover the banneton and place it in the fridge for 1 hour. This should now be early afternoon and you can decide whether you would like to bake the loaf for late afternoon or early evening.

Top Tip: If you prefer a more sour loaf and would therefore like to develop the flavor more in this dough, at step 5 leave the dough in the fridge for up to 24 hours. It will cease to be a same-day loaf, but it will create a stronger flavor.

Step 6: When you are ready to bake, decide whether you would like to bake in a preheated oven or from a cold start. If preheating, set the oven to 425°F (220°C) convection or 450°F (230°C) conventional. Remove the cover from the banneton, then place the parchment paper over the top of the banneton and put the pan upside down over the top of them both. With one hand under the banneton and one on the pan, turn it all over together to turn the dough out of the banneton and into the pan. Score the dome of dough.

Step 7: If you preheated the oven, put the lid on the pan or cover it with another cake tin or foil, and bake it for 40 minutes. If you are using a cold start, place the covered pan of dough in the oven, set the temperature as above and set a timer for 45 minutes. Remove the cover 10 minutes before the end of the baking time. After the full baking time, remove the pan from the oven. If you feel that it is looking pale, place the pan with the loaf back in the hot oven, minus the lid, for 5 to 10 minutes to brown the loaf to the color of your choice.

Step 8: Once it is baked, carefully remove the loaf from the pan, saving the parchment paper for next time, and allow the baked loaf to cool on a wire rack for at least an hour before slicing.

Same-Day Simplest Round Loaf

This loaf is not only made in a day, it also produces a super soft loaf. It does not include any tricky shaping and relies solely on the pan it is baked in to form its shape. It is one of the simplest loaves I make. If you are looking for a fast, relatively hands-off, soft, light and crusty loaf, this is it.

Equipment: An 8-inch (20-cm)-diameter cake tin with 3¾-inch (9.5-cm)-high sides, or a baking pan with a lid (or another cake tin or tin foil over the top), plus parchment paper or a cake tin liner.

Location: Use a warm place to proof the dough. I use my oven with the pilot light on and the door propped open, which creates an even temperature of 77°F (25°C). Alternatively, use a proofing box.

Makes 1 small loaf

100 g (½ cup) active starter

325 g (1⅓ cups) warm water, around 100°F (38°C)

500 g (4 cups) strong white bread flour

7 g (1 tsp) salt, or to taste

Step 1: In the morning, using a medium-sized mixing bowl, roughly mix together all the ingredients until you have a shaggy, rough dough. The dough will be sticky. Cover the bowl with a clean shower cap or your choice of cover and leave the bowl in your chosen warm spot.

Step 2: After half an hour, perform the first set of pulls and folds. Turn the bowl slightly and repeat this as many times as is necessary until the dough feels less sticky and comes together into a soft ball. This will be a warm and soft dough. Cover the bowl again and place it back in the warmth.

Step 3: After half an hour, perform the next set of pulls and folds, repeating the same actions again; the dough should be warm and stretchy, and it should come together into an easy ball. Place the covered bowl back in the warmth.

Step 4: After another half an hour, perform one last set of pulls and folds; the dough should come together into a nice, smooth, bouncy ball. Place the covered bowl back in the warmth for the next 3 hours, or until the dough has doubled in size.

Step 5: Once the dough is double its original size—it may be soft from the warm proofing—perform pulls and folds on the dough to form it into a nice ball. Place your hand over the whole dough and lift it out and place it smooth side up in the middle of your lined tin. Cover the tin and leave it on the counter to proof again and grow to double in size; the time this takes will depend on the room temperature in your kitchen so I advise watching the dough keenly to see when it has grown sufficiently. In my kitchen, this took 2 hours. The dough will spread and fill the pan.

Step 6: Once the dough has doubled in size again and is holding a soft dome shape, decide whether you would like to bake in a preheated oven or from a cold start. If preheating, set the oven to 400°F (200°C) convection or 425°F (220°C) conventional.

Step 7: If you preheated the oven, put the lid on the pan or cover it with another cake tin or foil, and bake it for 30 minutes. If you are using a cold start, place the covered pan of dough in the oven, set the temperature as above and set a timer for 35 minutes. Remove the cover 10 minutes before the end of the baking time. After the full baking time, remove the pan from the oven. If you feel that it is looking pale, place the pan with the loaf back in the hot oven, minus the lid, for 5 to 10 minutes to brown the loaf to the color of your choice.

Step 8: Once it is baked, carefully remove the loaf from the pan, saving the parchment paper for next time, and allow the baked loaf to cool on a wire rack for at least an hour before slicing.

Whole-Grain Spelt and Sesame Seed Enriched Dome

This loaf is made using an enriched dough made with sourdough starter and with added whole-grain spelt flour that gives the loaf a slight sweetness. Although the sesame seed top makes it look like a big burger bun, it is best sliced and shared! The sweetness of the loaf lends itself to be eaten with sweet or savory toppings; personally, I like to have slices with cream cheese or blue cheese.

Equipment: An 8-inch (20-cm)-diameter cake tin with 3¾-inch (9.5-cm)-high sides, or a baking pan with a lid (or another cake tin or tin foil over the top), plus parchment paper or a cake tin liner. This can also be baked in a loaf tin.

Makes 1 standard loaf

50 g (¼ cup) active starter

270 g (1⅛ cups) milk, cold or at room temperature (I use reduced-fat or 2% milk, but you can also use full-fat/whole milk)

2 large eggs (use 1 whole egg and 1 egg yolk in the dough, reserve the extra egg white for brushing)

75 g (¼ cup plus 2 tbsp) butter (I use slightly salted butter), at room temperature

50 g (¼ cup) runny honey

250 g (2 cups) strong white bread flour

250 g (2 cups) whole-grain/whole wheat spelt flour

7 g (1 tsp) salt, or to taste

Topping
20 g (2 tbsp) sesame seeds

Step 1: In the early evening, in a large mixing bowl, roughly mix together all the ingredients, except the reserved egg white and sesame seeds. It will be a sticky dough and it may be easier to use a bowl scraper or spatula to mix it at this stage. The butter will not be fully mixed through yet; it will become mixed in fully as you complete the next steps. Cover the bowl with a clean shower cap or your choice of cover and leave the bowl on the counter.

Step 2: After an hour, perform the first set of pulls and folds on the dough, lifting and pulling the dough across the bowl until it starts to come into a soft ball, then stop. During this first set of pulls and folds the dough will still be sticky but keep working with it. The butter will still not be fully mixed in yet; it will become more so as you work with the dough. Cover the bowl again and leave it to sit on the counter.

Step 3: During the next few hours, perform two more sets of pulls and folds on the dough, covering the bowl after each set. The dough will become nicely stretchy and will come together into a smooth, soft, whole-grain ball each time, and the aroma should be wonderful. Do the final set before going to bed.

Step 4: Leave the covered bowl on the counter overnight, typically 8 to 12 hours, at 64 to 68°F (18 to 20°C).

(continued)

Whole-Grain Spelt and Sesame Seed Enriched Dome (Continued)

Step 5: In the morning, hopefully the dough will have grown to double in size. If the dough has not doubled yet, allow it a few more hours to continue to proof. This is a heavy dough and may take longer than a standard water-based dough to fully proof.

Once the dough has fully grown, gently but firmly perform a final set of pulls and folds on the dough to pull it into a ball—it will be easy to handle—and place it smooth side up in the middle of your lined cake tin. Cover the tin with the same cover.

Allow the dough to proof again for 1 to 2 hours at room temperature, until it grows to double the size with a smooth domed top, filling the base of the tin.

Step 6: When you are ready to bake, decide whether you would like to bake in a preheated oven or from a cold start. Brush the surface of the loaf with the reserved egg white mixed with 15 grams (1 tbsp) of water, and sprinkle it with the sesame seeds.

If preheating, set the oven to 325°F (160°C) convection or 350°F (180°C) conventional.

Step 7: If you preheated the oven, bake it, covered, for 50 to 55 minutes. If you are using a cold start, place the covered tin of dough in the oven, set the temperature as above and set a timer for 55 to 60 minutes, or until it is nicely browned.

Step 8: Remove the loaf from the oven and tin, remove the parchment paper or liner and place it onto a wire rack to cool.

Top Tips: This loaf also works well using all whole wheat spelt flour. It is a heavier dough and produces a heavier loaf that has a sweetness and texture like cake.

Use the same dough and split it at step 6 to make rolls; it works perfectly! Follow the process used for the Milk Dinner Rolls (page 30), starting from step 5.

Pumpkin Spiced and Shaped Loaf

With its shape and the flavors I have included, this is a perfect loaf for fall. The baked loaf looks evocative and warm on any dinner table, but it can also be used to make a creatively shaped loaf for any time of the year for the sheer pleasure of serving up a fun and tasty loaf. I use butcher's twine to shape my dough and I have never had any issues with removing the twine once the loaf is baked; if you do have issues or use a different string, consider oiling the string to prevent sticking.

Equipment: A round banneton, 6¾ inches (17 cm) in diameter and 3¼ inches (8.5 cm) deep, or a lined bowl dusted with rice flour. Set aside an 8-inch (20-cm)-diameter cake tin with 3¾-inch (9.5-cm)-high sides, or a baking pan with a lid (or another cake tin or tin foil over the top), plus parchment paper or a cake tin liner. You will also need butcher's twine and a cinnamon stick or a stalk from a pepper, capsicum, squash or pumpkin.

Makes 1 small loaf

30 g (⅛ cup) active starter

100 g (½ cup) butternut squash puree

175 g (¾ cup) water

300 g (2½ cups) strong white bread flour

30 g (⅛ cup) roasted pumpkin seeds

50 g (⅓ cup) dried cranberries

4 g (1 tsp) pumpkin spice mix or "mixed spice" mix

4 g (1 tsp) salt, or to taste

Rice flour, for dusting

Step 1: In the early evening, in a large mixing bowl, roughly mix together all the ingredients, except the rice flour, until you have a shaggy, rough dough. Cover the bowl with a clean shower cap or your choice of cover and leave the bowl on the counter for 2 hours.

Step 2: After this rest time, perform the first set of pulls and folds until the dough feels less sticky and comes together into a firm ball. You will see and feel the puree, seeds and cranberries mixing through the dough. Cover the bowl again and leave it on your counter.

Step 3: After 1 to 1½ hours, do one more set of pulls and folds on the dough around the bowl and cover the dough again afterward.

Step 4: Leave the covered bowl on the counter overnight, typically 8 to 10 hours, at 64 to 68°F (18 to 20°C).

Step 5: In the morning, you should be greeted by a bowl full of grown, aromatic dough. Perform one last set of pulls and folds to form the dough into a nice ball. Place your hand over the whole dough and lift it into the banneton, smooth side down. Sprinkle extra rice flour down the sides and over the top of the dough. Cover the banneton and place it in the fridge for 3 to 24 hours.

(continued)

Pumpkin Spiced and Shaped Loaf (Continued)

Step 6: When you are ready to bake, decide whether you would like to bake in a preheated oven or from a cold start. If preheating, set the oven to 425°F (220°C) convection or 450°F (230°C) conventional.

Cut four pieces of string, each 28 inches (70 cm) long. Remove the cover from the banneton and with the dough still in the banneton, lay the strings evenly across it to create equal spaces over the dough, visually cutting the circle into eight equal portions. Place your parchment paper or pan liner over the top of the banneton and strings, and your pan over the top of both. Use both hands to turn it all over, keeping the strings firmly in place.

Remove the banneton and prepare to tie the strings. Making sure you are using the corresponding ends of each of the strings, pull each one over the dough and tie it firmly on the top. Allow the strings to slightly indent the dome of dough but do not pull them tightly into it. Tie the ends of the strings in bows so you will be able to undo them easily later. Score each segment of dough between the strings.

Step 7: If you preheated the oven, put the lid on the pan or cover it with another cake tin or foil, and bake it for 40 minutes. If you are using a cold start, place the covered pan of dough in the oven, set the temperature as above and set a timer for 45 minutes.

Once it is baked, remove the loaf carefully from the pan, place it on a rack and undo the strings. Place the loaf back into your pan and bake it, covered again, for a further 5 to 10 minutes to ensure it is baked through.

Step 8: Once it is baked, carefully remove the loaf from the pan, saving the parchment paper for next time, and allow the baked loaf to cool on a wire rack for at least an hour before slicing. Add a cinnamon stick or pepper/capsicum stalk for a fun presentation.

Top Tip: I use homemade butternut squash puree. You can also use homemade or store-bought pumpkin or sweet potato puree. My puree was nicely thick, not at all watery. If your puree is thinner you may need less water in the dough, or to bake it for longer to prevent the inside of the bread from being moist and gummy.

Fast Coconut and Cherry Tea Loaf

This loaf is for my beautiful boy. It is based on a cake he enjoys, so of course, I turned it into a sourdough version. This is a dense, heavy, cake-like loaf that can be enjoyed on its own, or with a layer of luscious butter or, for me, with a sharp cheese or tangy goat cheese. This is a fast recipe that uses sourdough starter for flavor rather than lift. In this recipe you can use unfed starter straight from the fridge, starter fed for this recipe or discard starter.

Equipment: An 8-inch (20-cm)-diameter cake tin with 3¾-inch (9.5-cm)-high sides, or a baking pan with a lid (or another cake tin or tin foil over the top), plus parchment paper or a cake tin liner. This can also be baked in a loaf tin.

Makes 1 standard loaf

100 g (½ cup) starter (fed, unfed or discarded)

400 g (1¾ cups) coconut milk

400 g (2½ cups) white spelt flour, plain or all-purpose flour

200 g (1¼ cups) glacé (candied) cherries

100 g (¾ cup) dried cranberries

50 g (½ cup) shredded coconut

30 g (⅛ cup) runny honey

1 large egg

7 g (1 tsp) baking soda

4 g (½ tsp) baking powder

Step 1: In a medium-sized mixing bowl, combine all the ingredients. Mix them well to form a lumpy, thick batter, ensuring no dry flour is left. It will fill the bowl.

Step 2: Spoon the mixture into your prepared loaf pan.

Step 3: When you are ready to bake, decide whether you would like to bake in a preheated oven or from a cold start. If preheating, set the oven to 350°F (180°C) for convection or 400°F (200°C) for conventional.

If you preheated the oven, bake the loaf uncovered for 50 to 60 minutes, or until a metal skewer or thin knife inserted into the center comes out clean. If you are using a cold start, place the uncovered pan of dough in the oven, set the temperature as above and set a timer for 60 minutes. Bake it for the allotted time, or until a metal skewer or thin knife inserted into the center comes out clean.

If the top of the loaf starts to overly brown, cover the pan with another pan upside down over the top, or with a piece of foil.

Step 4: Remove the pan from the oven and the loaf from the pan, removing the parchment paper or liner and placing it uncovered on a rack. Allow it to cool before serving.

Top Tip: Make a flax egg by mixing 7 grams (1 tbsp) of ground flaxseeds with 37 grams (2½ tbsp) of warm or room-temperature water. Stir, then allow it to sit for 5 minutes to thicken. Replace the egg with the flax egg.

Feta and Spinach Bundt Tin Loaf with Red Onion Topping

Bundt tins are a fun way to bake bread in different and unexpected styles and shapes. They produce a masterpiece worthy of discussion at any table! And as part of the fun, I like to pack these shapely loaves full of unexpected ingredients. This loaf marries a classic combination of feta cheese, spinach, nutmeg and red onion. The red onion slices added to the base of the tin roast and caramelize as the loaf bakes, infusing the loaf, and your kitchen, with the most amazing aroma. They also add a touch of sweetness to each slice.

Equipment: A 12-cup (2.8-L) Bundt tin, 10½ inches (27 cm) in diameter and 4½ inches (11.5 cm) deep. My Bundt tin is nonstick.

Makes 1 Bundt loaf

50 g (¼ cups) active starter

350 g (1½ cups) water

500 g (4 cups) strong white bread flour

7 g (1 tsp) salt, or to taste

Filling

25 g (¾ cup) fresh spinach leaves

2 g (1 tsp) nutmeg

125 g (¾ cup) feta, cut into small cubes, approximately ⅜ inch (1 cm)

Topping

½ medium red onion, cut into 2-mm slices

Step 1: In the early evening, in a large mixing bowl, roughly mix together all the ingredients, except the fillings and topping, until you have a shaggy, rough dough. Cover the bowl with a clean shower cap or your choice of cover and leave the bowl on the counter for 2 hours.

Step 2: After 2 hours, perform the first set of pulls and folds until the dough feels less sticky and comes together into a soft ball. Cover the bowl again and leave it on your counter.

Step 3: During the next few hours, do two more sets of pulls and folds on the dough, covering the dough after each set. Perform the final set before going to bed.

Step 4: Leave the covered bowl on the counter overnight, typically 8 to 10 hours, at 64 to 68°F (18 to 20°C).

(continued)

Feta and Spinach Bundt Tin Loaf with Red Onion Topping (Continued)

Step 5: In the morning, the dough will have grown to double, maybe almost triple, in size. My Bundt tin did not need to be greased; however, I recommend spraying it with a light layer of neutral oil, or greasing the inside of your Bundt tin with butter, if you know that your pan works best this way or it is a new tin that you have not used before.

Once the dough is two to three times its original size, turn it out onto a floured surface. Using your fingertips, gently push and stretch the dough out to a rectangle, 20 inches (50 cm) long and 4 inches (10 cm) wide. Spread the spinach leaves in a single layer over the dough. Sprinkle the nutmeg over the leaves, then place the cubes of feta cheese evenly over both. Next, roll one long side toward the other, pulling the dough into a fat sausage. Lay the slices of red onion inside the tin, in the wells of the shape. I use eight half slices of onion. Store the leftover onion for another use.

Lift the dough into the tin and, placing the smooth side down over the onion slices, shape it around the upright part in the middle of the pan. The dough should fit perfectly into the base of the pan. Try not to move it at this point as it will then move the onion pieces underneath it. The dough will grow to fill the space and close up the gap between the two ends of the dough. Cover the pan with the same cover you used earlier.

Allow the dough to proof again. It may not seem to grow much at this point due to the weight of the fillings, but allow it to puff up so that it looks like it has doubled in size. This may take 2 to 4 hours, depending on the temperature of your kitchen. The surface will become smooth and the dough will spread into the pan.

Step 6: When you are ready to bake, place parchment paper, followed by a baking sheet, on the top of the Bundt tin to serve as a lid. Decide whether you would like to bake in a preheated oven or from a cold start. To bake from a preheated oven, set the oven to 325°F (160°C) convection or 350°F (180°C) conventional.

Step 7: If you preheated the oven, bake it for 55 minutes. If you are baking from a cold start, set the temperature as above and bake it for 60 minutes.

Step 8: After the baking time, remove the loaf from the oven, then from the pan and allow it to cool on a wire rack briefly before slicing.

Blueberry Brioche-Style Bundt Tin Loaf

Imagine a brioche-style sourdough loaf with bursts of blueberries running through it—this is what this loaf will give you. Any blueberries that are touching the sides of the tin become jammy and gooey and are worth fighting for! This loaf is a great breakfast or supper loaf, and leftovers make an irresistible bread-and-butter pudding.

Brioche dough can be notoriously hard to work with due to the amount of butter included in the recipe, and usually requires a mixer for the job; in my enriched recipes I use less butter and mixing the butter through is far easier and does not require extra mechanical assistance.

As you handle the dough and pull and fold it through the early steps of the recipe, the butter mixes through the dough exactly as we need it to.

Equipment: I use my 10-cup (2.4-L) Bundt tin, 10¼ inches (26 cm) in diameter and 4 inches (10.5 cm) deep. This loaf will also work using a larger 12-cup (2.8-L) Bundt tin. My Bundt tin is nonstick.

Makes 1 Bundt loaf

100 g (½ cup) active starter

245 g (1 cup) milk, cold or at room temperature (I use reduced-fat or 2% milk, but you can also use full-fat/whole milk)

1 large egg

1 large egg yolk

75 g (¼ cup plus 2 tbsp) butter (I use slightly salted butter), at room temperature

50 g (¼ cup) runny honey

500 g (4 cups) strong white bread flour

7 g (1 tsp) salt, or to taste

Filling

250 g (1¼ cups) fresh blueberries

Step 1: In the early evening, in a large mixing bowl, roughly mix together all the ingredients, except the blueberries. It will be a sticky dough and it may be easier to use a bowl scraper or spatula to mix it at this stage. The butter will not be fully mixed through yet; it will become mixed in fully as you complete the next steps. Cover the bowl with a clean shower cap or your choice of cover and leave the bowl on the counter.

Step 2: After 2 hours of rest time, perform the first set of pulls and folds on the dough. During this first set of pulls and folds the dough will still be sticky but keep working with it. The butter will still not be fully mixed in yet; it will become more so as you work with the dough. Cover the bowl again and leave it to sit on the counter.

Step 3: After another 1 to 1½ hours, perform one more set of pulls and folds on the dough. The dough will remain sticky but nicely stretchy and will now come together into a nice smooth ball. Cover the bowl again and leave it on the counter.

Step 4: Leave the covered bowl on the counter overnight, typically 8 to 12 hours, at 64 to 68°F (18 to 20°C).

(continued)

Blueberry Brioche-Style Bundt Tin Loaf (Continued)

Step 5: In the morning, hopefully the dough will have grown to double in size. If the dough has not doubled yet, allow it a few more hours to continue to proof. This is a heavy dough and may take longer than a standard water-based dough to fully proof.

Have your Bundt tin ready. My Bundt tin did not need to be greased; however, I recommend spraying it with a light layer of neutral oil, or greasing the inside of your Bundt tin with butter, if you know that your pan works best this way or it is a new tin that you have not used before.

Once the dough is double its original size, place another clean mixing bowl on the counter and remove one-quarter of the dough (250 grams [9 oz]) from the main bowl and place it into the new bowl. Firmly perform a final set of pulls and folds on this smaller piece of dough to pull it into a ball. Lift the dough ball in your hand, and using your fingers, ease a hole into the middle of it, like a huge bagel. Place the dough into the Bundt pan, smooth side down, with the hole over the upright part in the middle of the pan and push it down to the bottom of the pan. Place 50 grams (¼ cup) of the blueberries on top, sticking them to the dough.

Next, remove a little less than half of the remainder (350 grams [12 oz]) of dough from the main bowl, and repeat the process again, placing the "bagel" of dough over the upright part in the middle of the Bundt tin and pushing it down on top of the blueberries and the first piece of dough. Cover this piece of dough with a little more than 50 grams (¼ cup) of blueberries, sticking them to the dough to hold them in place.

With the remaining dough, pull it into another ball, then make it into a "bagel" and place it over the top of the dough and berries in the tin. Place the remaining berries all over the surface of the dough so that you have a spotty dough and the three layers stacked on top of each other.

Cover the pan with the same cover. Allow the dough to proof again, letting it grow to double the size. This may take 2 to 4 hours, depending on the temperature of your kitchen.

Step 6: When you are ready to bake, decide whether you would like to bake in a preheated oven or from a cold start. Place parchment paper, followed by a baking sheet, on the top of the Bundt pan to serve as a lid. If preheating, set the oven to 325°F (160°C) convection or 350°F (180°C) conventional.

Top Tip: To hold the baking sheet in place over the Bundt tin, I place ceramic baking beads in it.

Step 7: If you preheated the oven, bake the loaf, covered, for 60 to 65 minutes. If you are using a cold start, place the covered pan of dough in the oven, set the temperature as above and set a timer for 65 to 70 minutes, or until it is nicely browned.

Step 8: Remove the tin from the oven and sit it on a rack with the loaf still inside it. Allow it to cool in the tin for 10 to 15 minutes. If during this time the loaf starts to sink while still sitting in the tin, put it back in the oven for 10 more minutes. If not, turn the loaf out onto a rack and allow it to cool. Serve it warm as it is, or drizzle it with melted chocolate before slicing into it as I did in the photograph.

Holiday Chocolates Enriched Bundt Tin Loaf

In our house, we end up with collections of chocolates from various holidays, so one day I decided to collect all of them, chop them into pieces and add them to an enriched dough featuring spelt flour. This is how this loaf was created and it was so good, I then made it five more times in two weeks!

The bread is so soft and light, and the added chopped chocolate pieces are spread evenly through the loaf, providing bursts of sweetness and a perfect treat. Eat it unadorned or with butter or sharp cheese. This loaf is a winner in our house.

Equipment: A 12-cup (2.8-L) Bundt tin, 10½ inches (27 cm) in diameter and 4½ inches (11.5 cm) deep. My Bundt tin is nonstick.

Makes 1 Bundt loaf

---

100 g (½ cup) active starter

350 g (1½ cups) oat milk, cold or at room temperature (you can also use reduced-fat or 2% milk, full-fat/whole milk)

50 g (¼ cup) butter (I use slightly salted butter), at room temperature

50 g (¼ cup) runny honey

350 g (2⅔ cups) strong white bread flour

150 g (1¼ cups) whole wheat spelt flour

200 g (1 cup) chopped chocolate (cut into halves or approximately ½-inch [1.3-cm] pieces, see Top Tips)

7 g (1 tsp) salt, or to taste

Step 1: In the early evening, in a large mixing bowl, roughly mix together all the ingredients. It will be a sticky, lumpy dough, and it may be easier to use a bowl scraper or spatula to mix it at this stage. The butter will not be fully mixed through yet; it will become mixed in fully as you complete the next steps. Cover the bowl with a clean shower cap or your choice of cover and leave the bowl on the counter.

Step 2: After 2 hours, perform the first set of pulls and folds on the dough, lifting and pulling the dough across the bowl until it starts to come into a soft ball, then stop. During this first set of pulls and folds the dough will still be sticky, studded with the chocolate pieces throughout, surrounded by dough that quickly becomes smooth. Cover the bowl again and leave it to sit on the counter.

Step 3: After another hour, perform another set of pulls and folds on the dough, covering the bowl afterward. This will be a big, smooth and stretchy dough studded with the chocolate pieces, and will come together into a soft ball. Cover the bowl again.

Step 4: Leave the covered bowl on the counter overnight, typically 8 to 12 hours, at 64 to 68°F (18 to 20°C).

(continued)

Step 5: In the morning, hopefully the dough will have grown to double in size. If the dough has not doubled yet, allow it a few more hours to continue to proof. This is a heavy dough and may take longer than a standard water-based dough to fully proof.

Have your Bundt tin ready. My Bundt tin did not need to be greased; however, I recommend spraying it with light layer of neutral oil, or greasing the inside of your Bundt tin with butter, if you know that your pan works best this way or it is a new tin that you have not used before.

Once the dough is two times its original size, gently but firmly perform a final set of pulls and folds on the dough to pull it into a ball. The dough will be big and bouncy and studded with chocolate pieces. Pick up the ball of dough in one hand and use your forefingers from your other hand to ease a hole into the middle of it. Next, place it smooth side down into the prepared Bundt pan, placing it over and tucking it around the upright part in the middle of the pan, and then cover it with the same shower cap. Allow the dough to proof again, letting it grow to approximately halfway up the side of the pan. This may take 2 to 4 hours, depending on the temperature of your kitchen. The dough will spread into the pan.

Step 6: When you are ready to bake, decide whether you would like to bake in a preheated oven or from a cold start. Place parchment paper, followed by a baking sheet, on the top of the Bundt pan to serve as a lid. If preheating, set the oven to 325°F (160°C) convection or 350°F (180°C) conventional.

Step 7: If you preheated the oven, bake the loaf, covered, for 55 to 60 minutes. If you are using a cold start, place the covered pan of dough in the oven, set the temperature as above and set a timer for 60 to 65 minutes, or until it is nicely browned.

Step 8: Remove the loaf from the oven, remove the baking sheet and paper, allow the loaf to cool for 5 minutes and then turn it out onto a wire rack to cool. If you would like the loaf to have more color, return it to the oven, on the rack, sitting on a baking sheet, and bake it uncovered for 5 to 10 minutes. Then remove it and let it cool before slicing.

Top Tips: I use leftover mini chocolate truffle eggs and various filled bars of chocolate. I have also made this recipe using chopped solid chocolate and chopped-up pieces of chocolate orange, all of which worked perfectly.

To hold the baking sheet in place over the Bundt tin, I place ceramic baking beads in it.

Gingerbread Cookie Enriched Bundt Tin Loaf

This loaf was created as a result of having a tin of leftover gingerbread cookies from Christmas. I decided to crush up some into a dough to see what would happen and the result was a very tasty loaf with the flavor of the cookies spread throughout. The cookies that I used were very thin and the ones added directly to the dough literally melted into it. The extra cookies added later in the process provide extra bursts of flavor to the cut loaf.

Equipment: A 12-cup (2.8-L) Bundt tin, 10½ inches (27 cm) in diameter and 4½ inches (11.5 cm) deep. My Bundt tin is nonstick.

Makes 1 Bundt loaf

100 g (½ cup) active starter

330 g (1¼ cups) milk, cold or at room temperature (I use reduced-fat or 2% milk, but you can also use full-fat/whole milk)

1 large egg

75 g (¼ cup plus 2 tbsp) butter (I use slightly salted butter), at room temperature

50 g (¼ cup) runny honey

500 g (4 cups) strong white bread flour

150 g (¾ cup) crushed gingerbread cookies

7 g (1 tsp) salt, or to taste

Filling

150 g (¾ cup) crushed gingerbread cookies

Step 1: In the early evening, in a large mixing bowl, roughly mix together all the ingredients, except the extra filling cookies. It will be a sticky dough and it may be easier to use a bowl scraper or spatula to mix it at this stage. The butter will not be fully mixed through yet; it will become mixed in fully as you complete the next steps. Cover the bowl with a clean shower cap or your choice of cover and leave the bowl on the counter.

Step 2: After an hour, perform the first set of pulls and folds on the dough. During this first set of pulls and folds, the dough will still be sticky but keep working with it. The butter will still not be fully mixed in yet; it will become more so as you work with the dough, and you may find that the cookies have already dissolved into the dough. Cover the bowl again and leave it to sit on the counter.

Step 3: After another hour, perform another set of pulls and folds on the dough, covering the bowl afterward. The dough will remain sticky but nicely stretchy and will come together into a soft ball. The aroma should be wonderful, and the dough will have become tinted with color from the cookies. Cover the bowl again.

Step 4: Leave the covered bowl on the counter overnight, typically 8 to 12 hours, at 64 to 68°F (18 to 20°C).

(continued)

Step 5: In the morning, hopefully the dough will have grown to double in size. If the dough has not doubled yet, allow it a few more hours to continue to proof. This is a heavy dough and may take longer than a standard water-based dough to fully proof.

Have your Bundt tin ready. My Bundt tin did not need to be greased; however, I recommend spraying it with a light layer of neutral oil, or greasing the inside of your Bundt tin with butter, if you know that your pan works best this way or it is a new tin that you have not used before.

Once the dough has doubled, turn it out onto a floured surface. Using your fingertips, gently push and stretch the dough out to a rectangle, 20 x 4 inches (50 x 10 cm). Sprinkle the remaining crushed cookies over the dough, then roll one long side toward the other, pulling the dough into a fat sausage. Lift the dough into the tin and, placing the smooth side down, shape it around the upright part in the middle of the pan. Cover the pan with the same cover you used earlier.

Allow the dough to proof again, letting it grow to 1 to 1½ inches (2.5 to 4 cm) lower than the edge of the pan. This may take 2 to 4 hours, depending on the temperature of your kitchen. The surface will become smooth and the dough will spread into the pan.

Step 6: When you are ready to bake, decide whether you would like to bake in a preheated oven or from a cold start. Place parchment paper, followed by a baking sheet, on the top of the Bundt pan to serve as a lid. If preheating, set the oven to 325°F (160°C) convection or 350°F (180°C) conventional.

Step 7: If you preheated the oven, bake the loaf, covered, for 55 to 60 minutes. If you are using a cold start, place the covered pan of dough in the oven, set the temperature as above and set a timer for 60 to 65 minutes, or until it is nicely browned.

Step 8: Remove the loaf from the oven, remove the baking sheet and paper, allow the loaf to cool for 5 minutes, then turn it out onto a wire rack to cool.

Top Tips: If you do not have gingerbread cookies, add 12 grams (2 tbsp) of pumpkin pie spice mix or gingerbread spice mix to the dough from step 1. Use crumbled cookies of your choice to fill the dough and to add some extra flavor and texture in step 5.

To hold the baking sheet in place over the Bundt tin, I place ceramic baking beads in it.

The Muffin Tin
COLLECTION

The Easiest Way to Bake Sourdough Rolls and Coils

Why should muffin pans be used for just cake-based muffins? Want to make the easiest uniformly shaped bread rolls? Take out that muffin pan and give it a new use! It provides the perfect support for evenly sized and shaped rolls. In this chapter, you will find a wide selection of flavor combinations, including apricot and apple; cheese and marmite; date and pistachio; sweet potato; apple and cheese; and pizza toppings all wrapped up in various doughs and baked in muffin tins.

The recipes in this chapter have all been made using my nonstick, standard 12-hole muffin tin. If you have metal, fluted brioche tins you can also use them for these recipes. The muffin tin I use has hollows that measure approximately 3 inches (7.5 cm) wide at the opening and taper to 2 inches (5 cm) wide at the bottom.

With all these recipes, once the doughs have been portioned, shaped and placed in the muffin tin, they can be baked immediately or the filled tin can be covered and placed in the fridge and baked directly from the fridge when you are ready.

Same-Day Baby Sourdough Rolls

Your muffin tin is perfect for making evenly shaped baby sourdough rolls. In this recipe, warmth is used to make the process faster and to produce rolls within the same day. Choose a warm place to proof your dough and watch it grow before your eyes!

Equipment: Have a 12-hole muffin tray ready, preferably nonstick. If your muffin tin is not nonstick, lightly spray or grease inside the wells with a neutral or flavorless oil or butter.

Location: Use a warm place to proof the dough. I use my oven with the pilot light on and the door propped open, which creates an even temperature of 77°F (25°C). Alternatively, use a proofing box.

Makes 12 small rolls

100 g (½ cup) active starter

325 g (1⅓ cups) warm water, around 100°F (38°C)

500 g (4 cups) strong white bread flour

7 g (1 tsp) salt, or to taste

Step 1: In a medium-sized mixing bowl, roughly mix together all the ingredients until you have a shaggy, rough dough. The dough will be sticky. Cover the bowl with a clean shower cap or your choice of cover and leave the bowl in your chosen warm spot.

Step 2: After half an hour, perform the first set of pulls and folds. Turn the bowl slightly and repeat this as many times as is necessary until the dough feels less sticky and comes together into a soft ball. This will be a warm, soft dough. Cover the bowl again and place it back in the warmth.

Step 3: After half an hour, perform the next set of pulls and folds, repeating the same actions again; the dough should be nice and stretchy and bouncy, and it should come together into a smooth, soft ball. Place the covered bowl back in the warmth.

Step 4: After another half an hour, perform the last set of pulls and folds; the dough should come together into a nice, smooth, bouncy ball. Place the covered bowl back in the warmth for the next 3 hours, or until the dough has doubled in size.

Step 5: Once the dough is double its original size —it may be soft from the warm proofing, but it should not be floppy—place the dough, untouched but still covered, in the fridge for half an hour. The dough will firm up, making it easier to work with.

When you are ready to shape the rolls, turn the dough out onto a floured surface. Using a dough knife or sharp knife, cut the dough into twelve pieces, 75 grams (2½ oz) each or as equal as you can get by eye. Shape each piece into a ball. Place the balls into the wells, smooth side up, then cover the whole pan with a large reusable plastic bag or a clean, damp tea towel, and allow them to proof again for 1½ to 2 hours, or until they are doubled in size.

Step 6: When you are ready to bake, decide whether you would like to bake in a preheated oven or from a cold start. If preheating, set the oven to 400°F (200°C) convection or 425°F (220°C) conventional.

Step 7: If you preheated the oven, bake the rolls uncovered for 16 to 18 minutes, or until they are nicely risen and starting to brown.

To bake from a cold start, place the uncovered pan of dough in the oven, set the temperature as directed and bake them for a total of 18 to 20 minutes, or until they are nicely risen and browning.

Step 8: Once they are baked, remove them from the oven and eat them once they are slightly cooled.

Apple and Apricot Enriched Sourdough "Roses"

These scrumptious rolls are made using my enriched dough filled with apricot jam and wrapped around softened apple slices. The beauty of using a muffin tin to make and bake these is that the tin helps to shape the rolls for you and to create the "roses."

Equipment: Have a 12-hole muffin tray ready, preferably nonstick. If your muffin tin is not nonstick, lightly spray or grease inside the wells with a neutral or flavorless oil or butter.

Makes 12 rolls

30 g (⅛ cup) active starter

200 g (¾ cup) milk, cold or at room temperature (I use reduced-fat or 2% milk, but you can also use full-fat/whole milk)

1 large egg

30 g (⅛ cup) salted butter, at room temperature

30 g (⅛ cup) runny honey

400 g (3¼ cups) strong white bread flour

7 g (1 tsp) salt, or to taste

Filling

3 small, sweet, red apples, peeled (100 g [3½ oz]) (I use Royal Gala apples)

100 g (½ cup) apricot jam

10 g (2 tsp) lemon juice, to prepare apples

Topping

Granulated sugar, vanilla or cinnamon sugar to sprinkle on top, optional

Step 1: In the early evening, in a large mixing bowl, roughly mix together all the ingredients, except the fillings and optional topping. It will be a ragged dough, and it may be easier to use a bowl scraper or spatula to mix it at this stage. The butter will not be fully mixed through yet; it will become mixed in fully as you complete the next steps. Cover the bowl with a clean shower cap or your choice of cover and leave the bowl on the counter.

Step 2: After 2 hours, perform the first set of pulls and folds on the dough, lifting and pulling the dough across the bowl until it starts to come into a soft ball, then stop. The butter will still not be fully mixed in yet, but will become more so as you work with the dough. During this first set of pulls and folds, the dough may still be sticky and quite stiff but stretchable.

Cover the bowl again and leave it to sit on the counter.

Step 3: After 1 to 1½ hours, perform another set of pulls and folds on the dough. The dough will remain slightly sticky but will be nicely stretchy and will come together into a soft, smooth ball.

Step 4: Leave the covered bowl on the counter overnight, typically 8 to 12 hours, at 64 to 68°F (18 to 20°C).

Step 5: In the morning, hopefully the dough will have grown to between double and triple in size, with a smooth surface. If the dough does not seem sufficiently proofed yet, allow it a few more hours to continue to proof. This is a heavy dough and may take longer than a standard water-based dough to fully proof.

Place the dough, untouched but still covered, in the fridge for at least an hour, until you are ready to use it. The dough will firm up, making it easier to work with later.

(continued)

Apple and Apricot Enriched Sourdough "Roses" (Continued)

Step 6: To make the apple roses, remove the cores from the apples and slice them into thin slices, a maximum of 1 to 2 mm thick. Place all the slices into a heat-proof bowl of water and add the lemon juice, ensuring that the water covers all the slices. Microwave them on high, uncovered, for 5 minutes, or until the slices are soft and pliable. Once softened, tip the apple slices into a colander to drain and cool them.

Meanwhile, turn the dough out onto a floured surface and using a rolling pin, roll it out to a rectangle, 24 x 10 inches (60 x 26 cm). This dough will behave like pastry and can be rolled and handled the same way.

Cut the dough into 12 strips, each 2 inches (5 cm) wide. Spread 10 grams (2 tsp) of jam along each strip.

To make the roses, place 5 slices of apple along a strip of the dough, with the apple peel edges level with the edge of the strip of dough, leaving 1 inch (2.5 cm) clear at each end. With your first strip of dough, fold one of the uncovered ends over the first apple slice, then continue to roll the dough and apples up from one end to the other. Place the rolled-up dough rose into the muffin tin with the apple slices pointing upward. Repeat with all the strips.

Once all the roses have been made, cover the filled muffin tin with a damp tea towel or large plastic bag and let them rest at room temperature for 1 hour.

Step 7: When you are ready to bake, decide whether you would like to bake in a preheated oven or from a cold start. If preheating, set the oven to 350°F (180°C) convection or 400°F (200°C) conventional. If you are choosing to, sprinkle the roses with sugar before placing the tin in the oven.

If you preheated the oven, bake them uncovered for 30 minutes. If you are using a cold start, place the filled muffin pan in the cold oven, set the temperature as above and set a timer for 35 minutes.

Step 8: Once they are baked, remove the pan from the oven, carefully remove the roses and let them sit briefly on a rack before serving. They are best eaten freshly baked.

Top Tip: Store leftovers in an airtight container for up to 3 days and heat them for 30 to 60 seconds in the microwave to enjoy within that time.

Sweet Potato, Apple and Cheese Roll Ups

This is a wholly indulgent recipe as it brings together so many of my favorites—my sweet potato dough wrapped around roasted chunks of apple and tasty strong cheese, all baked into easy-to-eat snack-size rolls. The sharpness of the mature cheese cuts through the sweetness from the apple and sweet potato to create a perfect marriage in each mouthful. The dough is designed to be easily handled and baked in a muffin tray for absolute ease from start to finish.

Equipment: Have a 12-hole muffin tray ready, preferably nonstick. If your muffin tin is not nonstick, lightly spray or grease inside the wells with a neutral or flavorless oil or butter.

Makes 12 rolls

50 g (¼ cup) active starter

150 g (6 oz) mashed, cooked and cooled sweet potato

280 g (1 cup) water

400 g (2¾ cups) strong white bread flour

7 g (1 tsp) salt, or to taste

Filling

150 g (¾ cup) roasted apple chunks (see Top Tip)

125 g (1 cup) grated strong flavored cheese, for example, farmhouse mature Cheddar, strong double Gloucester, cave-aged hard goat cheese or similar

Step 1: In the early evening, in a large mixing bowl, roughly mix together all the ingredients, except the apple and cheese, leaving the dough shaggy. Cover the bowl with a clean shower cap or your choice of cover and leave it on the counter for 2 hours.

Step 2: After this resting time, perform the first set of pulls and folds on the dough; it will be sticky and possibly stiff at this point, but stretchy. Cover the bowl and leave it on the counter.

Step 3: After another hour, complete one more set of pulls and folds on the dough. The dough will be nicely stretchy and will easily come together into a soft, now-orange ball. Cover the bowl again.

Step 4: Leave the covered bowl on the counter overnight, typically 8 to 10 hours, at 64 to 68°F (18 to 20°C).

Step 5: The next morning, the dough will be doubled in size. Place the dough, untouched but still covered, in the fridge for at least an hour, until you are ready to use it. The dough will firm up, making it easier to work with later.

(continued)

Sweet Potato, Apple and Cheese Roll Ups (Continued)

Step 6: When you are ready to bake, decide whether you would like to bake in a preheated oven or from a cold start. If preheating, set the oven to 400°F (200°C) convection or 425°F (220°C) conventional. If your muffin tin is not nonstick, lightly spray or grease inside the wells with butter or a neutral or flavorless oil.

Take your bowl of dough from the fridge. Sprinkle flour over your kitchen counter. Using a bowl scraper or your hands, gently ease the bubbly risen dough from the bowl onto the counter. Use your fingertips to start stretching and pushing out the dough, until it becomes a rectangle that measures 18 x 12 inches (45 x 30 cm) with an even thickness all over. The dough will want to pull back as you stretch it; continue to pull it gently, careful not to make holes in the dough. If the dough starts to tear or seems very hard to stretch, let it rest on the counter for 5 to 10 minutes, allowing the gluten in the dough to relax and try again.

Spread the apple pieces evenly all over the stretched dough and sprinkle the grated cheese evenly over the top, right up to the edges. Roll up the dough from one of the longer edges toward the other to make an even, tight roll of dough. Using a dough knife or sharp knife, cut the dough into twelve equal pieces, approximately 1½ inches (4 cm) wide. Place them, cut side down, in the muffin pan hollows. If the coils start to fall apart, or you struggle with the dough holding together, push them into the pan hollows however they come. Do not worry about perfect shaping; the muffin pan will create the roll shapes for you as they bake.

Step 7: If you preheated the oven, bake them uncovered for 25 minutes. If you are using a cold start, place the filled muffin pan in the cold oven, set the temperature as above and set a timer for 30 minutes.

Step 8: Once they are baked, remove the pan from the oven, carefully remove the roll ups and let them sit briefly on a rack before serving. These are best eaten freshly baked, but my testers tell me that they were also still very tasty reheated for 30 to 60 seconds in the microwave a few days later.

Top Tip: To make the roasted apple chunks, I use 3 medium apples (350 grams [11½ oz] before coring, 300 grams [10 oz] after coring), cut into chunks, with the skin left on. Place the chunks of raw apple on a baking sheet and roast them at 400°F (200°C) convection or 425°F (220°C) conventional for 30 to 35 minutes until they are browned, soft and starting to caramelize. Cool them before adding them to the dough.

Stuffed Pizza Rolls

These pizza rolls are made using one of my favorite processes—stretching out my dough after the main overnight proof, covering it with my favorite ingredients, rolling it up, chopping it up and baking the pieces into filled rolls. In this recipe, I have updated my process and use a standard muffin tray to bake the rolls. This works perfectly to provide a uniform size but also helps to shape the rolls. It means that even if the dough gets messy or hard to handle, you can stuff it into the muffin spaces and it will still bake up beautifully to even-sized muffin-shaped rolls.

Equipment: Have a 12-hole muffin tray ready, preferably nonstick. If your muffin tin is not nonstick, lightly spray or grease inside the wells with a neutral or flavorless oil or butter.

Makes 12 roll ups

50 g (¼ cup) active starter

325 g (1⅓ cups) water

500 g (4 cups) strong white bread flour

7 g (1 tsp) salt, or to taste

Filling

150 g (¾ cup) pizza sauce

200 g (2 cups) grated cheese (I use hard "pizza mozzarella" that I can grate. You can also use a mix of mozzarella and Monterey Jack)

Additional pizza toppings of your choice (for example, thinly cut mushrooms or sliced meats such as pepperoni or chorizo [avoid anything too thick or chunky])

Step 1: In the early evening, in a large mixing bowl, roughly mix together all the ingredients, except the pizza sauce, cheese and any other filling ingredients, leaving the dough shaggy. Cover the bowl with a clean shower cap or your choice of cover and leave it on the counter for 2 hours.

Step 2: After the 2 hours, perform the first set of pulls and folds on the dough; it will be sticky at this point, but stretchy. Cover the bowl and leave it on the counter.

Step 3: Once the dough has rested for at least an hour, complete two more sets of pulls and folds on the dough throughout the evening, covering the bowl after each set. The dough will be nicely stretchy and will easily come together into a firm ball each time. Complete the final set before going to bed.

Step 4: Leave the covered bowl on the counter overnight, typically 8 to 10 hours, at 64 to 68°F (18 to 20°C).

Step 5: The next morning, place the dough, untouched but still covered, in the fridge for at least an hour, until you are ready to use it; this could be for lunch, dinner or a meal the next day. The dough will firm up, making it easier to work with later.

(continued)

Stuffed Pizza Rolls (Continued)

Step 6: When you are ready to bake, decide whether you would like to bake in a preheated oven or from a cold start. If preheating, set the oven to 400°F (200°C) convection or 425°F (220°C) conventional.

Take your bowl of dough from the fridge. Sprinkle flour over your kitchen counter. Using a bowl scraper or your hands, gently ease the bubbly risen dough from the bowl onto the counter. Use your fingertips to start stretching and pushing out the dough, until it becomes a rectangle that measures 18 x 12 inches (45 x 30 cm) with an even thickness all over. The dough will want to pull back as you stretch it; continue to pull it gently, careful not to make holes in the dough. If the dough starts to tear or seems very hard to stretch, let it rest on the counter for 5 to 10 minutes, allowing the gluten in the dough to relax and try again.

Spread the pizza sauce evenly all over the stretched dough and sprinkle the grated cheese evenly over the top, right up to the edges. If you are adding extra fillings, place them over the sauce and cheese. Roll up the dough from one of the longer edges toward the other to make an even, tight roll of dough. Using a dough knife or sharp knife, cut the dough into twelve equal pieces, approximately 1½ inches (4 cm) wide. Place them, cut side down, in the muffin pan hollows. If the rolled up portions of filled dough start to fall apart, or you struggle with the dough holding together, push them into the pan hollows however they come. Do not worry about perfect shaping; the muffin pan will create the roll shapes for you as they bake.

Step 7: If you preheated the oven, bake the rolls uncovered for 25 minutes. If you are using a cold start, place the filled muffin pan in the cold oven, set the temperature as above and set a timer for 30 minutes.

Step 8: Once they are baked, remove the pan from the oven, carefully remove the rolls and let them sit briefly on a rack before serving. They are best eaten freshly baked, but my testers also informed me that they were still great eaten a few days later and reheated in a microwave for 30 seconds.

Top Tip: If you would prefer to bake them later, follow step 6 to fill, roll and cut up the dough into pieces, and then place the rolls into the muffin tin. Cover the tin with a large plastic bag or damp tea towel and place it in the fridge. When you are ready to bake, you can bake them directly from the fridge, following the directions above.

Date Paste, Pistachio and Cocoa Roll Ups

These mini treats are made using a chocolate dough filled with date paste and ground pistachio nuts. You may be tempted to try one straight from the oven, but from experience, I can tell you that they taste better if you can make yourself wait. Once cooled you will be able to fully appreciate the flavors in the dough and from the fillings. If you do not have pistachio nuts available, use any ground nuts of your choice. If you prefer an alternative to the date paste, try fig, raisin or prune paste or honey.

Equipment: Have a 12-hole muffin tray ready, preferably nonstick. If your muffin tin is not nonstick, lightly spray or grease inside the wells with a neutral or flavorless oil or butter.

Makes 12 baby roll ups

30 g (⅛ cup) active starter

180 g (¾ cup) water

50 g (¼ cup) runny honey

300 g (2½ cups) strong white bread flour

20 g (3 tbsp) cocoa powder

4 g (½ tsp salt), or to taste

Filling

120 g (½ cup) date paste (see Top Tips)

30 g (⅛ cup) ground unsalted pistachios

Step 1: In the early evening, in a large mixing bowl, roughly mix together all the ingredients, except the fillings, leaving the dough shaggy. Cover the bowl with a clean shower cap or your choice of cover and leave it on the counter for 2 hours.

Step 2: After this rest time, perform the first set of pulls and folds on the dough; this will be a small, stiff dough and may be easy to fold over itself in the bowl at this point. Cover the bowl and leave it on the counter.

Step 3: After 1 to 1½ hours, do one more set of pulls and folds on the dough, covering the dough again afterward. It will continue to be stiff, now stretchier, almost fully chocolate colored and smelling wonderful.

Step 4: Leave the covered bowl on the counter overnight, typically 8 to 10 hours, at 64 to 68°F (18 to 20°C).

Step 5: The next morning, the dough will be a puffy, aromatic, smooth ball of chocolate dough and will be ready to be used to make the rolls. It will be slightly stiff and firm and easy to handle.

(continued)

Date Paste, Pistachio and Cocoa Roll Ups (Continued)

Step 6: When you are ready to bake, decide whether you would like to bake in a preheated oven or from a cold start. If preheating, set the oven to 400°F (200°C) convection or 425°F (220°C) conventional.

Sprinkle flour over your kitchen counter. Using a bowl scraper or your hands, gently ease the bubbly risen dough from the bowl onto the counter. Use your fingertips to start stretching and pushing out the dough until it becomes a rectangle that measures 12 x 10 inches (30 x 26 cm) with an even thickness all over. The dough will want to pull back as you stretch it; continue to pull it gently, careful not to make holes in the dough. If the dough starts to tear or seems very hard to stretch, let it rest on the counter for 5 to 10 minutes to allow the gluten in the dough to relax and try again.

Spread the date paste evenly all over the dough, then sprinkle it with the ground pistachios, right up to the edges. Roll up the dough from one of the longer edges toward the other to make an even, tight roll of dough. Using a dough knife or sharp knife, cut the dough into twelve equal pieces, approximately 1 inch (2.5 cm) wide. Place them, cut side down, in the muffin pan hollows. If the coils start to fall apart, or you struggle with the dough holding together, push them into the pan hollows however they come. Do not worry about perfect shaping; the muffin pan will create the roll shapes for you as they bake.

Step 7: If you preheated the oven, bake them uncovered for 25 minutes. If you are using a cold start, place the filled muffin pan in the cold oven, set the temperature as above and set a timer for 30 minutes.

Step 8: Once they are baked, remove the pan from the oven, carefully remove the rolls and let them sit briefly on a rack before serving. They are best eaten once cooled so that you can fully taste the flavors.

Top Tips: If you cannot find date paste, it can easily be made by blending pitted dates with a small amount of water.

If you would prefer to bake them later, follow step 6 to fill, roll and cut up the dough into pieces and then place the coils into the muffin tin. Cover the tin with a large plastic bag or damp tea towel and place it in the fridge. When you are ready to bake, you can bake them directly from the fridge, following the directions above.

Milk and Honey Braided Knots

The dough for these knots includes milk and honey, making it silky and easy to work with and shape into whatever form you fancy, not to mention lending a delicious, delicate flavor to the loaf once baked. For these, I have braided the portions of dough, then rolled them up to make small, inviting rolls that are then brushed with egg, which makes them browned and shiny, and can then be sprinkled with seeds before baking to create different looks.

Equipment: Have a 12-hole muffin tray ready, preferably nonstick. If your muffin tin is not nonstick, lightly spray or grease inside the wells with a neutral or flavorless oil or butter.

Makes 12 rolls

30 g (⅛ cup) active starter

200 g (¾ cup) milk

20 g (2 tbsp) runny honey

300 g (2½ cups) strong white bread flour

4 g (½ tsp salt), or to taste

1 large egg, for brushing

Seeds to sprinkle over the rolls before baking (optional; I use poppy seeds, golden flaxseeds and sesame seeds)

Step 1: In the early evening, in a large mixing bowl, roughly mix together all the ingredients except the egg and seeds, leaving the dough shaggy. Cover the bowl with a clean shower cap or your choice of cover and leave it on the counter for 2 hours.

Step 2: After this rest time, perform the first set of pulls and folds on the dough; it will be stiff from the milk, and it may be easier to fold over itself than to pull and stretch. Cover the bowl and leave it on the counter.

Step 3: After 1 more hour, complete one more set of pulls and folds on the dough, covering the bowl again afterward. The dough will be stretchier now and will easily come together into a smooth, firm ball.

Step 4: Leave the covered bowl on the counter overnight, typically 8 to 10 hours, at 64 to 68°F (18 to 20°C).

Step 5: The next morning, the dough will be ready to make the rolls. The dough can be used immediately, or you can place the dough, untouched but still covered, in the fridge for an hour, or until you are ready to use it; this could be for lunch, dinner or breakfast the next day.

Step 6: When you are ready to make the rolls, turn the dough out onto a floured surface and use a dough knife or sharp knife to cut it into twelve portions, each weighing 45 grams (1½ oz). Cut each individual portion equally into two, so you have 24 portions, and roll the pieces between your hands to create 24 strands, each approximately 5 inches (13 cm) long.

To make the rolls, pinch the ends of two strands together, twist them around each other, then twist the whole piece around itself to make a braided round. Place them into the muffin tin wells. Once all the rolls have been made, cover the tin with a damp tea towel or plastic bag and let them rest at room temperature for 1 to 2 hours, or until they are doubled in size.

Top Tip: If you would prefer to bake them later, follow step 6 to make the rolls and place them into the muffin tin. Cover the tin with a large plastic bag or damp tea towel and place it in the fridge. When you are ready to bake, you can bake them directly from the fridge, following the directions to the right.

Step 7: When you are ready to bake, decide whether you would like to bake in a preheated oven or from a cold start. If preheating, set the oven to 350°F (180°C) convection or 400°F (200°C) conventional.

Whisk the egg in a small bowl and brush the egg wash over each roll. Sprinkle them with seeds if you are using them.

If you preheated the oven, bake them uncovered for 20 minutes. If you are using a cold start, place the filled muffin pan in the cold oven, set the temperature as above and set a timer for 25 minutes.

Step 8: Once they are baked, remove the pan from the oven, carefully remove the rolls and let them sit briefly on a rack before serving. These are best eaten freshly baked.

Cheese and Marmite Coils

Cheese and marmite is a partnership made in the stars, in mine and my son's opinion. The flavors balance one another to create a perfect marriage. If marmite is new to you, it has a unique salty, umami flavor, and a little goes a long way. Try it in this recipe, but also try a thin layer over your buttered toast, or add it to soup, stews or curries for an added depth of flavor. These rolls are bite-size as the flavors are quite strong, but we also love bigger versions if you fancy scaling up the size.

Equipment: Have a 12-hole muffin tray ready, preferably nonstick. If your muffin tin is not nonstick, lightly spray or grease inside the wells with a neutral or flavorless oil or butter.

Makes 12 small coiled rolls

30 g (⅛ cup) active starter

210 g (¾ cup plus 2 tbsp) water

300 g (2½ cups) strong white bread flour

30 g (⅛ cup) flaxseeds

4 g (½ tsp salt), or to taste

Filling

30 g (⅛ cup) marmite mixed with 10 g (1 tbsp) warm water to make it easier to drizzle

150 g (1½ cups) grated cheese (I use mature Red Leicester, but you can use any full-flavored hard cheese that melts well and teams up with the umami flavor of the marmite such as aged Cheddar, Gouda or Gouda)

Step 1: In the early evening, in a large mixing bowl, roughly mix together all the ingredients, except the marmite and cheese, leaving the dough shaggy. Cover the bowl with a clean shower cap or your choice of cover and leave it on the counter for 2 hours.

Step 2: After this time, perform the first set of pulls and folds on the dough; it will be stretchy and studded with the seeds. Cover the bowl and leave it on the counter.

Step 3: After an hour, complete one more set of pulls and folds on the dough, covering the bowl afterward. The dough will be nicely stretchy and will easily come together into a firm ball each time. I aim to do this final set before going to bed.

Step 4: Leave the covered bowl on the counter overnight, typically 8 to 10 hours, at 64 to 68°F (18 to 20°C).

Step 5: The next morning, place the dough, untouched but still covered, in the fridge for at least an hour, until you are ready to use it; this could be for lunch, dinner or breakfast the next day. In the fridge, the dough will firm up, making it easier to work with later.

(continued)

Cheese and Marmite Coils (Continued)

Step 6: When you are ready to bake, decide whether you would like to bake in a preheated oven or from a cold start. If preheating, set the oven to 400°F (200°C) convection or 425°F (220°C) conventional.

Take your bowl of dough from the fridge. Sprinkle flour over your kitchen counter. Using a bowl scraper or your hands, gently ease the bubbly risen dough from the bowl onto the counter. Use your fingertips to start stretching and pushing out the dough, until it becomes a rectangle that measures 16 x 9 inches (40 x 23 cm) with an even thickness all over. The dough will want to pull back as you stretch it; continue to pull it gently, careful not to make holes in the dough. If the dough starts to tear or seems very hard to stretch, let it rest on the counter for 5 to 10 minutes, allowing the gluten in the dough to relax and try again.

Spread the watered-down marmite all over the dough, up to the edges. Sprinkle the cheese evenly over the top. Roll up the dough from one of the longer edges toward the other to make an even, tight roll of dough. Using a dough knife or sharp knife, cut the dough into twelve equal pieces, 1¼ inches (3 cm) wide. Place them, cut side down, in the muffin pan hollows. If the coils start to fall apart, or you struggle with the dough holding together, push them into the pan hollows however they come. Do not worry about perfect shaping; the muffin pan will create the roll shapes for you as they bake.

Step 7: If you preheated the oven, bake them uncovered for 25 minutes. If you are using a cold start, place the filled muffin pan in the cold oven, set the temperature as above and set a timer for 30 minutes.

Step 8: Once they are baked, remove the pan from the oven, carefully remove the rolls and let them sit briefly on a rack before serving. They are best eaten freshly baked.

Top Tip: If you would prefer to bake them later, follow step 6 to fill, roll and cut up the dough into pieces, and then place the coils into the muffin tin. Cover the tin with a large plastic bag or damp tea towel and place it in the fridge. When you are ready to bake, you can bake them directly from the fridge, following the directions above.

Sweet Potato, Za'atar and Tahini Rolls

If you like the idea of filled rolls that are not only packed with flavor, but also can be served as part of a vegan meal, these are ideal. I created these for a vegan visitor and the baked sweet potato flesh spreads to a smooth consistency, making it a perfect filling. The addition of za'atar and tahini renders them thoroughly irresistible.

To make the filling, I baked two medium sweet potatoes (about 400 grams [14 oz]) whole until they were tender. Once cooled, I scraped out the flesh into a bowl without breaking it up. The baked flesh can then be spread across the dough without needing to puree or mash it.

Equipment: Have a 12-hole muffin tray ready, preferably nonstick. If your muffin tin is not nonstick, lightly spray or grease inside the wells with a neutral or flavorless oil or butter.

Makes 12 rolls

50 g (¼ cup) active starter

350 g (1½ cups) water

300 g (2½ cups) strong white bread flour

200 g (2 cups) whole wheat flour

7 g (1 tsp) salt, or to taste

Fillings

200 g (7 oz) cooked sweet potato flesh

18 g (2 tbsp) za'atar

70 g (¼ cup) tahini (I use Middle Eastern tahini that is thin enough to drizzle)

Step 1: In the early evening, in a large mixing bowl, roughly mix together all the ingredients, except the fillings, leaving the dough shaggy. Cover the bowl with a clean shower cap or your choice of cover and leave it on the counter for 2 hours.

Step 2: After the rest time, perform the first set of pulls and folds on the dough; it will be sticky at this point, but stretchy. Cover the bowl and leave it on the counter.

Step 3: After 1 more hour, complete one more set of pulls and folds on the dough, covering the bowl afterward. The dough will be nicely stretchy and will easily come together into a firm ball.

Step 4: Leave the covered bowl on the counter overnight, typically 8 to 10 hours, at 64 to 68°F (18 to 20°C).

Step 5: The next morning, place the dough, untouched but still covered, in the fridge for at least an hour, until you are ready to use it; this could be for lunch, dinner or breakfast the next day. In the fridge, the dough will firm up, making it easier to work with later.

(continued)

Sweet Potato, Za'atar and Tahini Rolls (Continued)

Step 6: When you are ready to bake, decide whether you would like to bake in a preheated oven or from a cold start. If preheating, set the oven to 400°F (200°C) convection or 425°F (220°C) conventional.

Take your bowl of dough from the fridge. Sprinkle flour over your kitchen counter. Using a bowl scraper or your hands, gently ease the bubbly risen dough from the bowl onto the counter. Use your fingertips to start stretching and pushing out the dough, until it becomes a rectangle that measures 18 x 12 inches (45 x 30 cm) with an even thickness all over. The dough will want to pull back as you stretch it; continue to pull it gently, careful not to make holes in the dough. If the dough starts to tear or seems very hard to stretch, let it rest on the counter for 5 to 10 minutes, allowing the gluten in the dough to relax and try again.

Spread the cooked sweet potato flesh evenly all over the stretched dough; it will spread like a paste. Sprinkle the za'atar evenly over the potato, then drizzle with the tahini, right up to the edges. Roll up the dough from one of the longer edges toward the other to make an even, tight roll of dough. Using a dough knife or sharp knife, cut the dough into twelve equal pieces, approximately 1½ inches (4 cm) wide. Place them, cut side down, in the muffin pan hollows. If the coils start to fall apart, or you struggle with the dough holding together, push them into the pan hollows however they come. Do not worry about perfect shaping; the muffin pan will create the roll shapes for you as they bake.

Step 7: If you preheated the oven, bake them uncovered for 25 minutes. If you are using a cold start, place the filled muffin pan in the cold oven, set the temperature as above and set a timer for 30 minutes.

Step 8: Once they are baked, remove the pan from the oven, carefully remove the rolls and let them sit briefly on a rack before serving. These are wonderful eaten freshly baked, but if you can resist and eat them after a few hours or the next day, the flavors develop even more.

Top Tip: If you would prefer to bake the rolls later, follow step 6 to fill, roll and cut up the dough into pieces, and then place the coils into the muffin tin. Cover the tin with a large plastic bag or damp tea towel and place it in the fridge. When you are ready to bake, you can bake them directly from the fridge, following the directions above.

Falafel-Spiced Chickpea Bites

These bites are made with all the flavors and many of the ingredients you would find in a falafel recipe. This is a fast recipe in which the sourdough starter provides flavor and texture, not lift. When baked they have a crispy shell and soft middle and are absolutely divine eaten fresh, as soon as they are cool enough to handle. Having said that, the flavors also develop more over a few hours and days, and are just as good reheated. They also freeze and defrost well. Try dipping them into soup or dips, or eat them on their own when they are freshly baked as a tasty snack.

Equipment: Have a 12-hole muffin tray ready, preferably nonstick. If your muffin tin is not nonstick, lightly spray or grease inside the wells with a neutral or flavorless oil or butter.

Makes 12 scone-sized "bites"

100 g (½ cup) starter

125 g (½ cup plus 2 tbsp) milk

100 g (½ cup) plain flour

200 g (2 cups) besan/chickpea flour

1 large egg

4 g (2 tsp) tabil spice mix (equal quantities of ground cumin, coriander and caraway)

2 g (1 tsp) Aleppo pepper

7 g (1 tsp) salt

7 g (2 tsp) baking powder

30 g (¼ cup) chopped fresh parsley

30 g (⅛ cup) olive oil

Step 1: In a medium-sized mixing bowl, combine all the ingredients. Mix them well to form a thick, gluey batter, ensuring no dry flour is left.

Step 2: Spray a small amount of neutral oil into each well of your muffin tin. Spoon the mixture evenly between the 12 spaces.

Step 3: When you are ready to bake, decide whether you would like to bake in a preheated oven or from a cold start. If preheating, set the oven to 400°F (200°C) for convection or 425°F (220°C) for conventional.

If you preheated the oven, bake them uncovered for 10 to 12 minutes. If you are using a cold start, set the temperature as above and set a timer for 15 minutes.

Step 4: Remove the pan from the oven and place the bites on a rack briefly. Serve them either warm or cooled.

Top Tips: The flavors develop even more with time. To eat the bites at a later date, store them in an airtight container once they are fully cooled. When you are ready to eat them, reheat them briefly in the oven for 5 to 10 minutes at 350°F (180°C) convection or 400°F (200°C) conventional.

Alternatively, freeze the bites once they are fully cooled, and to serve, defrost them uncovered on a wire rack, then reheat them in the oven for 5 to 10 minutes at 350°F (180°C) convection or 400°F (200°C) conventional.

The Oven Tray
COLLECTION

Using Sourdough to Create Wonderful Breads with Built-In Simplicity

Sourdough can be so many things. Once you have the dough made, you can shape it, fill it, chop it, roll it, coil it . . . the possibilities are endless. In this chapter, I am sharing lots of my creations featuring one of the most versatile tools in your kitchen: a simple baking sheet. I will show you how easy it is to use a baking sheet to make everything from sourdough braided loaves, flatbreads and flavored focaccia to filled breads and baked egg bread boats.

These recipes also include some rolls and provide an alternative way of baking them from those baked in a covered pan in The Bread Pan Collection earlier in the book to show a slightly different process and outcome. Both processes work and can be interchanged.

Top Tip: In all the following recipes, after the main or overnight proof, if you would like to bake the dough later in the day, place the bowl, untouched and still covered with the fully proofed dough inside, in the fridge to halt any more growth. When you are ready to use the dough, take it from the fridge, allow it to warm up on the counter for about an hour and then continue from step 5.

Same-Day Goat Cheese and Spice Seeded Braid

This bread creation is made using a simple dough infused with spices and seeds, and with goat cheese folded into it after proofing. It makes a large, family-sized loaf that will adorn any table and make a great addition to a meal.

Equipment: A large baking sheet (mine is approximately 12 x 16 inches [30 x 41 cm]), lined with parchment paper.

Location: Use a warm place to proof the dough. I use my oven with the pilot light on and the door propped open, which creates an even temperature of 77°F (25°C). Alternatively, use a proofing box.

Makes 1 loaf

---

100 g (½ cup) active starter

325 g (1⅓ cups) warm water, around 100°F (38°C)

500 g (4 cups) strong white bread flour

50 g (¼ cup) roasted golden flaxseeds

14 g (2 tbsp) "bravas" spice mix (see Top Tips)

7 g (1 tsp) salt, or to taste

Filling

125 g (1 cup) roughly crumbled goat cheese, for example Chèvre, or full-fat cream cheese

---

Step 1: In a medium-sized mixing bowl, roughly mix together all the ingredients, except the goat cheese, until you have a shaggy, rough and sticky dough. Cover the bowl with a clean shower cap or your choice of cover and leave the bowl in your chosen warm spot.

Step 2: After half an hour, perform the first set of pulls and folds. This will be a warm, soft dough but the spices and seeds will help to firm it up. Cover the bowl again and place it back in the warmth.

Step 3: After half an hour, perform the next set of pulls and folds, repeating the same actions again. The dough should be nice and stretchy and will smell amazing, and it should come together into a smooth, soft ball. Place the covered bowl back in the warmth.

Step 4: After another half an hour, perform the last set of pulls and folds; the dough should come together into a nice, smooth, bouncy ball. Place the covered bowl back in the warmth for the next 3 hours, or until the dough has doubled in size.

Step 5: Once the dough is double its original size, place the dough, still in the bowl, covered and untouched, in the fridge for 30 to 60 minutes.

Step 6: When you are ready to bake, decide whether you would like to bake in a preheated oven or from a cold start. If preheating, set the oven to 400°F (200°C) convection or 425°F (220°C) conventional.

Take the dough from the fridge, using it while it is still cold, and using a bowl scraper or your hands, gently ease the dough from the bowl onto the counter. Use your fingertips to start stretching and pushing out the dough, until it becomes a 9 x 15–inch (22 x 40–cm) rectangle with an even thickness all over. The dough will want to pull back as you stretch it; continue to pull it gently, being careful not to make holes in the dough.

Top Tips: My spice mix is a store-bought mix that contains salt, garlic, sweet smoked paprika, cayenne and oregano. You can use something similar, make up your own version or use your favorite mix.

If you leave the loaf to cool or eat it the next day, the flavors will develop further. Eat it as it is or reheat it briefly in the oven for 5 to 10 minutes at 350°F (180°C) convection or 400°F (200°C) conventional.

Spread the crumbled goat cheese all over the dough. Roll up the dough from one of the longer edges toward the other to make an even roll of dough. Once rolled, use a dough knife or sharp knife to cut the sausage lengthwise down the middle into two equal pieces. Twist the two pieces together, then lift the whole dough onto your lined pan.

Step 7: If you preheated the oven, bake the loaf uncovered for 25 to 30 minutes, or until it is nicely risen and starting to brown.

To bake it from a cold start, place the uncovered pan of dough in the oven, set the temperature as directed and bake it for a total of 30 to 35 minutes, or until it is nicely risen and starting to brown.

Step 8: Once it is baked, remove the braid from the oven and eat it once it is slightly cooled.

Same-Day Cheats Baguettes

This is a method I use weekly to make "baguette style" breads for my household and it works so well that I felt it should be shared. This method requires no special shaping, no linen cloches, no special pans, just a simple process of making the dough, proofing it in an oval banneton, then tipping it out, cutting it up and baking it. And every time it produces wonderfully light, airy breads.

Equipment: An 11-inch (28-cm) oval banneton sprinkled with rice flour. Set aside a large baking sheet (mine is approximately 12 x 16 inches [30 x 41 cm]), lined with parchment paper.

Location: Use a warm place to proof the dough. I use my oven with the pilot light on and the door propped open, which creates an even temperature of 77°F (25°C). Alternatively, use a proofing box.

Makes 4 baguettes

100 g (½ cup) active starter

325 g (1⅓ cups) warm water, around 100°F (38°C)

500 g (4 cups) strong white bread flour

7 g (1 tsp) salt, or to taste

Rice flour for dusting

Step 1: In the morning, using a medium-sized mixing bowl, roughly mix together all the ingredients, except the rice flour, until you have a shaggy, rough dough. The dough will be sticky. Cover the bowl with a clean shower cap or your choice of cover and leave the bowl in your chosen warm spot.

Step 2: After half an hour, perform the first set of pulls and folds until the dough feels less sticky and comes together into a soft ball. This will be a warm and soft dough. Cover the bowl again and place it back in the warmth.

Step 3: After half an hour, perform the next set of pulls and folds; the dough should be warm and stretchy, and it should come together into an easy ball. Place the covered bowl back in the warmth.

Step 4: After another 30 minutes, perform the last set of pulls and folds; the dough should now come together into a nice, smooth, bouncy ball. Place the covered bowl back in the warmth for the next 3 hours, or until the dough has doubled in size.

Step 5: Once the dough has doubled, sprinkle an extra layer of rice flour into your banneton. To place the dough in the oval banneton, lift and pull the dough over itself along one side of the bowl. Turn the bowl 180 degrees and pull the dough on that side again in a line to create a fat sausage of dough. Place the dough, smooth side down, in the banneton, sprinkling extra rice flour down the sides and across the top of the dough, cover it again with the same shower cap and place it in the fridge for 3 hours.

Step 6: When you are ready to bake, decide whether you would like to bake in a preheated oven or from a cold start. If preheating, set the oven to 400°F (200°C) convection or 425°F (220°C) conventional.

Top Tip: These also freeze and defrost perfectly. Freeze them once they are fully cooled. To defrost them, place the baguettes uncovered on a wire rack for an hour. In my kitchen, the baguettes defrost with crisp crusts, just as if they have been freshly baked. If yours are soft, the baguettes can be refreshed by placing them on a baking sheet and into the oven at 350°F (180°C) convection or 400°F (200°C) conventional for 5 to 10 minutes to crisp them up again.

Have your lined baking sheet ready. Remove the banneton from the fridge, take off the cover from the banneton and sprinkle your work surface with flour. Gently turn over the banneton to turn the dough out onto the counter. With a dough knife or sharp knife, cut the formed dough cleanly in half right down the middle lengthwise. Cut each half in half again down the middle lengthwise so that you have four lengths of dough. Place each one carefully onto your baking sheet, slightly stretching them out as you place them.

Step 7: If you preheated the oven, bake them uncovered for 20 minutes. If you are using a cold start, place the uncovered baking sheet in the oven, set the temperature as directed and set a timer for 25 minutes.

Step 8: Once they are baked, carefully remove the baking sheet, saving the parchment paper for next time, and place the baguettes on a wire rack briefly. You can eat them once they have cooled slightly.

Seeded Pide with Cheese, Red Pepper and Baked Eggs

These dough "boats" are filled with sliced red pepper, chopped baby tomatoes, Cheddar and mozzarella, with an option to top them with an egg, making them a meal all by themselves. I add some salad and dips on the side for a perfect feast. I use the dough to make four smaller breads, or you can make two larger versions.

Equipment: A large baking sheet (mine is approximately 12 x 16 inches [30 x 41 cm]), lined with parchment paper.

Makes 4 small breads

30 g (⅛ cup) active starter

100 g (½ cup) water

120 g (½ cup + 1 tbsp) milk, cold or at room temperature (I use reduced-fat or 2% milk, but you can also use full-fat/whole milk or plant-based milk)

20 g (1 tbsp) flaxseeds

300 g (2½ cups) strong white bread flour

7 g (1 tsp) salt, or to taste

Toppings

¼ long sweet red pepper, sliced thinly

6 baby/piccolo tomatoes, quartered

50 g (¼ cup) grated medium Cheddar cheese

125 g (1 cup) thinly sliced fresh mozzarella

4 medium to large eggs

Aleppo chili flakes to sprinkle on top (optional)

Step 1: In the early evening, in a large mixing bowl, roughly mix together all the ingredients, except the toppings, until you have a shaggy, rough dough. Cover the bowl with a clean shower cap or your choice of cover and leave the bowl on the counter for 2 hours.

Step 2: After the rest time, perform the first set of pulls and folds, lifting and stretching portions of the dough up and over the bowl, turning the bowl continuously to perform them evenly around the whole dough. The dough will be stiff from the milk and the seeds. Cover the bowl again and leave it on your counter for 1 more hour.

Step 3: After the hour, do another set of pulls and folds on the dough; it will be stretchier now and will easily come into a firm, seed-studded ball. Cover the bowl again.

Step 4: Leave the covered bowl on the counter overnight, typically 8 to 10 hours, at 64 to 68°F (18 to 20°C).

Step 5: The next morning, the dough will have doubled in size and is now ready to be used to make the dough "boats." You can use the dough immediately, or if you would like to make the pide later in the day, place the dough untouched and still covered in the fridge. When you are ready to use it, take it from the fridge and use it directly.

Step 6: When you are ready to bake, decide whether you would like to bake in a preheated oven or from a cold start. If preheating, set the oven to 350°F (180°C) convection or 400°F (200°C) conventional.

Have your lined baking sheet ready. Turn the dough out onto a floured surface. Cut it into four even pieces. Roll each piece into a ball and then form each one into an oval shape, approximately 3 x 6 inches (7.5 x 15 cm). Place the ovals onto the lined baking sheet and divide the cheeses, red pepper and tomatoes between the four pieces, spreading them across the oval pieces and leaving a clear uncovered ¾-inch (2-cm) edge all the way around. Fold the edges in and pinch the ends together. Bake them for 18 minutes from a preheated start or 20 minutes from a cold start.

Step 7: After this time, remove the pan from the oven, crack an egg into each "boat" and bake them for a further 4 to 5 minutes, or until the egg whites are set but the yolks are still runny.

Step 8: Remove the baking sheet from the oven and serve them immediately. Sprinkle them with Aleppo chili flakes or pul biber to serve, if desired.

Top Tips: Try a mix of Cheddar, Asiago and mozzarella cheeses, or your favorite pizza topping cheeses.

To serve without the added eggs, bake it for 20 to 22 minutes each until the cheese is bubbling and browning.

Same-Day Mana'eesh Flatbreads with Za'atar, Olive Oil and Cheese

These flavorful flatbreads are hugely evocative for me as they remind me so much of my childhood spent living in the Middle East. These are my sourdough versions of these traditional "pizzas." They can be topped with just the za'atar and olive mixture, or with the added cheese, too. I highly recommend trying out both versions and seeing which you prefer. Eat them on their own warm, with salads and dips or alongside a main meal.

Equipment: 2 large baking sheets (mine are approximately 12 x 16 inches [30 x 41 cm]).

Location: Use a warm place to proof the dough. I use my oven with the pilot light on and the door propped open, which creates an even temperature of 77°F (25°C). Alternatively, use a proofing box.

Makes 2 breads

60 g (¼ cup plus 1 tbsp) active starter

200 g (¾ cup) warm water, around 100°F (38°C)

300 g (2½ cups) strong white bread flour, plus more for dusting

4 g (½ tsp salt), or to taste

Rice flour or semolina flour

Topping
30–45 g (2–3 tbsp) olive oil

30 g (2 tbsp) za'atar

60 g (½ cup) grated cheese (optional; I use a strong hard Cheddar, but you can also use mozzarella or scamorza smoked mozzarella)

Step 1: In a medium-sized mixing bowl, roughly mix together all the ingredients, except the rice or semolina flour and your toppings, until you have a shaggy, rough dough. The dough will be sticky. Cover the bowl with a clean shower cap or your choice of cover and leave the bowl in your chosen warm spot.

Step 2: After half an hour, perform the first set of pulls and folds until the dough comes together into a soft ball. This will be a warm, soft dough. Cover the bowl again and place it back in the warmth.

Step 3: After half an hour, perform the next set of pulls and folds; the dough should be nice and stretchy and bouncy, and it should come together into a smooth, soft ball. Place the covered bowl back in the warmth.

Step 4: After one final half an hour, perform the last set of pulls and folds; the dough should come together into a nice, smooth, bouncy ball. Place the covered bowl back in the warmth for the next 3 hours, or until the dough has doubled in size.

Step 5: Once the dough is double its original size, prepare your baking sheets by sprinkling them with a layer of rice flour or ground semolina.

Using a bowl scraper or your hands, gently ease the bubbly risen dough from the bowl onto a floured surface. Split the dough into two equal pieces and shape both pieces into balls. Let the balls sit on the counter for 10 minutes to rest.

Step 6: After this time, place the balls on the prepared pans, and use your fingertips to push and pull the dough balls into flat ovals approximately 8 x 16 inches (20 x 40 cm) each and about ¼ inch (6 mm) thick. Mix the za'atar with the olive oil and spoon it evenly over both ovals, right up to the edges. Sprinkle them with cheese, if using.

Step 7: When you are ready to bake, decide whether you would like to bake them in a preheated oven or from a cold start. If preheating, set the oven to 425°F (220°C) convection or 450°F (230°C) conventional. Bake them for 12 to 15 minutes from a preheated start, or 15 to 18 minutes from a cold start, or until the cheese is melted and browned and the base is cooked and crisp.

Step 8: Remove the flatbreads from the oven and serve them while they are hot and fresh.

Butternut Squash, Pecan and Fall Spiced Focaccia

This holey, pillowy sourdough focaccia is studded with the flavors and colors of fall, the time of year that I like the best. The spices are added to the dough from the start to build flavor as the dough proofs, and the chunks of butternut squash and pecans are added just before baking. Thus, as the bread bakes, the squash becomes slightly charred on the edges and the pecans toast and get satisfyingly crunchy. I roasted a whole large butternut squash and pureed half of it to make the Pumpkin Spiced and Shaped Loaf on page 99; the other half I cut into chunks for this recipe.

Other ideas are to roast a large squash for dinner one night, saving 200 grams (7 oz) for this recipe, or to simply roast a small squash expressly for this focaccia.

Equipment: A medium-sized baking sheet with a raised rim/edge, about 10 x 14 inches (26 x 36 cm).

Makes 1 standard loaf

50 g (¼ cup) active starter

350 g (1½ cups) water

500 g (4 cups) strong white bread flour

7 g (1 tsp) pumpkin spice mix, or mixed spice mix

7 g (1 tsp) salt, or to taste

30–45 g (2–3 tbsp) olive oil, for drizzling

Topping

50 g (¼ cup) or 25 whole pecans

200 g (1¾ cups) or 25 pieces of cooked and cooled chunks of butternut squash, cut into about 1-inch (2.5-cm) cubes

Step 1: In the early evening, in a large mixing bowl, roughly mix together all the ingredients, except the toppings, nuts and olive oil, until you have a shaggy, rough dough. Cover the bowl with a clean shower cap or your choice of cover and leave the bowl on the counter for 2 hours.

Step 2: After this rest time, perform the first set of pulls and folds until the dough feels less sticky and comes together into a ball. It will feel quite stiff from the spices. Cover the bowl again and leave it on your counter.

Step 3: After another hour, perform one more set of pulls and folds on the dough until it comes into a firm ball, covering the bowl again afterward.

Step 4: Leave the covered bowl on the counter overnight, typically 8 to 10 hours, at 64 to 68°F (18 to 20°C).

Step 5: The next morning, the dough should have doubled in size. Please note that if your spice mix includes cinnamon, this can slow down how the dough proofs so if the dough has not yet doubled in size, allow it more time to fully do so. Once doubled, either use it immediately or if you would like to bake the dough later in the day, place the bowl, untouched but still covered with the proofed dough inside, in the fridge to halt any more growth. When you are ready to use the dough, take it from the fridge, allow it to warm up, then continue.

Prepare your baking sheet by liberally drizzling it with the olive oil. Using a bowl scraper or your hands, gently ease the bubbly risen dough from the bowl onto the prepared pan, being careful not to squash the dough too much. Gently turn it over in the oil so that it is covered completely. Cover the entire pan loosely with a large plastic bag or plastic wrap and leave it on the counter for 1½ to 2 hours, or until it has become puffy and visually doubled in size again.

Top Tip: You can replace the butternut squash with chunks of pumpkin or sweet potato.

Step 6: When you are ready to bake, decide whether you would like to bake in a preheated oven or from a cold start. If preheating, set the oven to 400°F (200°C) convection or 425°F (220°C) conventional.

Step 7: Using your fingertips, firmly press dimples all over the dough, spreading it out at the same time until it fills the pan. Push the chunks of butternut squash and pecans randomly into the dough.

If you preheated the oven, bake the focaccia uncovered for 20 minutes. If you are using a cold start, place the uncovered pan of dough in the oven, set the temperature as above and set a timer for 25 minutes.

Step 8: Remove the baked focaccia from the oven and let it rest in the pan for 15 to 20 minutes, then ease the baked bread off the pan, transfer it to a board or large plate, cut it into pieces and serve.

The Oven Tray Collection   153

Hasselback Garlic-Butter Grainy Rolls

The dough used for these rolls includes a portion of cooked grains, making it one of my favorite dough creations. Sourdough always responds well to grains in the mix, growing beautifully, and the grains add a satisfying chew to each mouthful. Enjoy these rolls as they are or cut and fill them with garlic butter to serve alongside a meal of your choice.

Equipment: A large baking sheet (mine is approximately 12 x 16 inches [30 x 41 cm]), lined with parchment paper. You will also need tin foil, for the latter part of the process.

Makes 6 medium rolls

50 g (¼ cup) active starter

350 g (1½ cups) water

500 g (4 cups) strong white bread flour

150 g (¾ cup) cooked and cooled grains (I use spelt grains [see Top Tip])

7 g (1 tsp) salt, or to taste

Rice flour for dusting

Filling

75 g (¼ cup plus 2 tbsp) garlic butter (can be store-bought or homemade)

Step 1: In the early evening, in a large mixing bowl, roughly mix together all the ingredients, except the rice flour and garlic butter, leaving the dough shaggy. Cover the bowl with a clean shower cap or your choice of cover and leave the bowl on the counter for 2 hours.

Step 2: After the rest time, perform the first set of pulls and folds. The dough will be stretchy, studded with grains and easy to work with at this point, and will come into an easy soft ball. Cover the bowl again and leave it on your counter for 1 more hour.

Step 3: After the hour, do another set of pulls and folds on the dough. It will be even stretchier now and will easily come into a ball. Cover the bowl again.

Step 4: Leave the covered bowl on the counter overnight, typically 8 to 10 hours, at 64 to 68°F (18 to 20°C).

Step 5: The next morning, the dough should have grown to double in size. Place the dough, untouched but still covered, in the fridge for at least an hour, until you are ready to use it; this could be for lunch, dinner or a meal the next day. The dough will firm up in the cold, making it easier to work with later.

When you are ready to shape the rolls, turn the cold dough out onto a floured surface. Using a dough knife or sharp knife, cut the dough into six pieces, 150 grams (5 oz) each or as equal as you can get by eye. Shape each piece into a ball, then roll them into mini baguette-shaped rolls, each one 7 inches (18 cm) long. Place the rolls onto the lined baking sheet, smooth side up, then cover the entire pan with a large reusable plastic bag or a clean, damp tea towel. Allow them to proof again for 1½ to 2 hours, or until they have doubled in size.

Top Tip: I love spelt grains in this dough, but it also works perfectly with cooked and cooled einkorn, emmer or khorason grains, rye berries or oat groats.

Step 6: When you are ready to bake, decide whether you would like to bake in a preheated oven or from a cold start. If preheating, set the oven to 400°F (200°C) convection or 425°F (220°C) conventional.

Step 7: If you preheated the oven, bake them uncovered for 20 minutes. If you are using a cold start, place the uncovered pan in the cold oven, set the temperature as above and set a timer for 25 minutes.

Step 8: Once they are baked, remove the pan from the oven and let it sit briefly on the counter. Once it is cool enough to handle, make 15 cuts across each roll, ¼ inch (6 mm) apart, but not slicing through the entire roll. Fill the slots with garlic butter, and wrap them all in a large piece of tin foil, then place it on the baking sheet again and return it to the oven for another 20 minutes, until the butter has melted and the rolls have browned. Carefully remove the hot rolls from the oven and serve.

Dukkah-Filled Braid

Dukkah is an aromatic Middle Eastern condiment made from nuts, sesame seeds and spices. I make my own, but you can find it online or in some food stores, too. By making your own you can choose inclusions of your choice, which is what I like to do. Adding dukkah to the dough brings fantastic flavor and texture to the bread and also helps to tighten up the dough, making it easy to handle.

Equipment: A medium-sized baking sheet, about 10 x 14 inches (26 x 36 cm), lined with parchment paper.

Makes 1 medium loaf

30 g (⅛ cup) active starter

210 g (1 cup) water

30 g (⅛ cup) olive oil

300 g (2½ cups) strong white bread flour, plus more for dusting

50 g (¼ cup) dukkah, homemade (see Top Tips for recipe) or store-bought

7 g (1 tsp) salt, or to taste (see Top Tips)

Rice flour, for dusting

Step 1: In the early evening, in a large mixing bowl, roughly mix together all the ingredients, except the rice flour, leaving the dough shaggy. Cover the bowl with a clean shower cap or your choice of cover and leave the bowl on the counter for 2 hours.

Step 2: After the rest time, perform the first set of pulls and folds. The dough will be stretchy and easy to work with at this point, and will come into a soft, aromatic ball. Cover the bowl again and leave it on your counter for 1 more hour.

Step 3: After the hour, do another set of pulls and folds on the dough. It will be stretchier now and will easily come into a ball with the dukkah spreading through it. Cover the bowl again.

Step 4: Leave the covered bowl on the counter overnight, typically 8 to 10 hours, at 64 to 68°F (18 to 20°C).

Step 5: The next morning, the dough will have grown to double in size. Place the dough, untouched but still covered, in the fridge for at least an hour, until you are ready to use it; this could be for lunch, dinner or a meal the next day. The dough will firm up in the cold, making it easier to work with later.

When you are ready to make the braid, turn the cold dough out onto a floured surface. Using a dough knife or sharp knife, cut the dough into three pieces and roll them out to 18-inch (46-cm) strands.

Braid them together to make a single braided loaf. Carefully lift the loaf and place it onto the lined baking sheet.

You can now bake this immediately, or if you are not ready to bake it yet, cover it and allow it to proof again at room temperature for 1 to 2 hours, either option works well. You can also cover and place the baking sheet in the fridge for 3 to 24 hours until you would like to bake it. When you are ready, bake it directly from the fridge.

Step 6: When you are ready to bake, decide whether you would like to bake in a preheated oven or from a cold start. If preheating, set the oven to 400°F (200°C) convection or 425°F (220°C) conventional.

Step 7: If you preheated the oven, bake the braid uncovered for 20 to 25 minutes, or until it is nicely risen and starting to brown.

To bake it from a cold start, place the uncovered pan of dough in the oven, set the temperature as directed and bake it for a total of 25 to 30 minutes, or until it is nicely risen and browning.

Step 8: Once it is baked, remove the braid from the oven and eat it once it is slightly cooled. If you leave the bread to fully cool, the flavors will develop more.

Top Tips: Some dukkah mixes can be quite salty. If yours is, you may not need to add the full amount of salt to the dough.

To make your own dukkah, add 50 grams (½ cup) of roasted hazelnuts, 25 grams (¼ cup) of toasted sesame seeds, 1 teaspoon of ground coriander and 1 teaspoon of cumin seeds with a pinch of salt to a blender and pulse them to a crumb, but not too fine. Consider adding some carraway seeds, fennel, chili flakes or other herbs and spices of your choice.

Same-Day Simple Rustic Rolls

These swirly rolls are fun to make with a unique look; each one is rustically individual. These are made by cutting up a proofed dough, coiling the pieces into swirls and then sprinkling them with the seeds of your choice. They bake to light and airy rolls ideal for serving to guests with soup, or just slathering with lots of butter!

Equipment: An 11-inch (28-cm) oval banneton sprinkled with rice flour. Set aside a large baking sheet (mine is approximately 12 x 16 inches [30 x 41 cm]), lined with parchment paper.

Location: Use a warm place to proof the dough. I use my oven with the pilot light on and the door propped open, which creates an even temperature of 77°F (25°C). Alternatively, use a proofing box.

Makes 12 rolls

100 g (½ cup) active starter

325 g (1⅓ cups) warm water, around 100°F (38°C)

500 g (4 cups) strong white bread flour

7 g (1 tsp) salt, or to taste

Rice flour for dusting

Poppy seeds or sesame seeds, for sprinkling on top

Step 1: In the morning, in a medium-sized mixing bowl, roughly mix together all the ingredients, except the rice flour and seeds, until you have a shaggy, rough dough. The dough will be sticky. Cover the bowl with a clean shower cap or your choice of cover and leave the bowl in your chosen warm spot.

Step 2: After half an hour, perform the first set of pulls and folds until the dough feels less sticky and comes together into a soft ball. This will be a warm and soft dough. Cover the bowl again and place it back in the warmth.

Step 3: After half an hour, perform the next set of pulls and folds, repeating the same actions again; the dough should be warm and stretchy, and it should come together into an easy ball. Place the covered bowl back in the warmth.

Step 4: After another half an hour, perform the last set of pulls and folds; the dough should come together into a nice, smooth, bouncy ball. Place the covered bowl back in the warmth for the next 3 hours, or until the dough has doubled in size.

Step 5: Once the dough has doubled, sprinkle an extra layer of rice flour into your banneton. To place the dough in the oval banneton, lift and pull the dough over itself along one side of the bowl. Turn the bowl around 180 degrees and pull the dough on that side again in a line to create a fat sausage of dough. Place the dough, smooth side down, in the banneton, sprinkling extra rice flour down the sides and across the top of the dough, cover it again with the same shower cap and place it in the fridge for 3 hours.

Step 6: When you are ready to bake, decide whether you would like to bake in a preheated oven or from a cold start. If preheating, set the oven to 400°F (200°C) convection or 425°F (220°C) conventional.

Have your lined baking sheet ready. Remove the banneton from the fridge, take off the cover from the banneton and sprinkle your work surface with flour. Gently turn over the banneton to turn the dough out onto the counter. With a dough knife or sharp knife, cut the formed dough cleanly in half right down the middle widthwise. Cut each half portion into six equal strips of dough. Sprinkle the pieces with your chosen seeds, then coil each piece to make a swirl shape. Place each one carefully onto your lined baking sheet.

Step 7: If you preheated the oven, bake the rolls uncovered for 18 minutes. If you are using a cold start, place the uncovered baking sheet in the oven, set the temperature as directed and set a timer for 20 minutes. After this time if you would prefer the rolls to be more browned, bake them for a further 2 to 5 minutes.

Step 8: Once they are baked, carefully remove the baking sheet, saving the parchment paper for next time. Place the rolls on a wire rack briefly and eat them once they are cooled slightly.

Spiced Cheese Sandwich Crackers

If I eat snacks I prefer to make them myself, and these crackers are a perfect snack. This recipe uses my sourdough cracker recipe from my first cookbook as a base with added spices. To create the cracker "sandwiches," we add a layer of cheese in between the cracker dough before baking. These crackers are best eaten when they have cooled slightly after baking, while they are still warm and fresh, but they can also be stored in an airtight container and crisped up again in the oven.

Equipment: 2 large baking sheets (mine are approximately 12 x 16 inches [30 x 41 cm]), both lined with parchment paper.

Makes 64 small crackers

200 g (1 cup) starter (fed, unfed or discard)

100 g (scant 1 cup) rolled oats

100 g (scant 1 cup) whole wheat flour, plus more for dusting

80 g (½ cup) seed mix (see Top Tip)

50 g (¼ cup) water

60 g (4 tbsp) olive oil

30 g (3 tsp) runny honey or pure maple syrup

14 g (2 tbsp) spice mix of your choice (I use a chip seasoning mix)

7 g (1 tsp) salt, or to taste

Sandwich Filling

200 g (7 oz) hard cheese, in 1 to 2 mm-thick slices (choose a cheese that melts without completely disintegrating; I use Cheddar, Red Leicester or a Mexican spiced cheese)

Step 1: In a medium-sized mixing bowl, mix together all the ingredients except the cheese to form a stiff dough. Ensure that the ingredients are well and evenly combined. Cover the bowl with a clean shower cap or your choice of cover and leave it on the counter overnight. The dough will grow and puff up slightly overnight, but it will not have a huge rise and does not need to.

Step 2: When you are ready to bake, decide whether you would like to bake in a preheated oven or from a cold start. If preheating, set the oven to 400°F (200°C) convection or 425°F (220°C) conventional.

Dust your kitchen counter with a little flour, turn the dough out onto the counter and use a rolling pin to roll the dough out to a 24 x 12–inch (60 x 30–cm) rectangle. Flour your rolling pin to prevent it from sticking and move your dough around as you roll it out so that it does not stick to the counter. Cut across the rectangle widthwise to make two equal halves. Place the cheese slices on one of the rectangles, covering the entire area. Lift the other half of the dough and place it on top of the cheese.

Using a pizza cutter or sharp knife, cut the dough into 1½-inch (4-cm) squares. If you would like larger crackers, cut the dough into bigger squares. Place the crackers on the prepared baking pan.

They can be placed close as they do not spread sideways as they bake.

Step 3: If you preheated the oven, bake them for 10 minutes on one side, remove the pan from the oven, turn over each cracker with a fork and a small metal spatula, return the pan to the oven, then bake them for another 10 minutes.

To bake them from a cold start, bake them for 12 minutes on each side.

Top Tip: I use 30 grams (⅛ cup) of sunflower seeds, 30 grams (⅛ cup) of millet seeds and 20 grams (2 tbsp) of poppy seeds in my seed mix.

Step 4: Remove the crackers from the oven and transfer them to a wire rack to cool slightly. They will crisp up as they cool. Store any leftovers in an airtight container.

Serve them as soon as they are cool enough to eat!

Bonus Recipe: Air Fryer Pitas

If you have an air fryer, these are so much fun to make. The dough puffs up into perfect pockets inside your machine. If you do not have an air fryer, these bread pockets can be baked in an oven instead. This recipe produces baby pitas, perfect for filling and eating immediately, or you can store them to eat the following day.

Equipment: An air fryer.

Makes 10 baby pitas

30 g (⅛ cup) active starter

180 g (scant ¾ cup) water

30 g (3 tbsp) olive oil

300 g (2½ cups) strong white bread flour, plus more for dusting

4 g (½ tsp) salt, or to taste

Step 1: In the early evening, in a medium-sized mixing bowl, roughly mix together all the ingredients until you have a shaggy, rough dough. This will be a small dough. Cover the bowl with a clean shower cap or your choice of cover and leave the bowl on the counter for about 2 hours.

Step 2: After the 2 hours, perform the first set of pulls and folds until the dough feels less sticky and comes together into a soft ball. The dough will be stretchy and easy to handle. Cover the bowl again and leave it on your counter.

Step 3: After 1 more hour, do one more set of pulls and folds on the dough, pulling it into a smooth, easy ball. Cover the bowl again.

Step 4: Leave the covered bowl on the counter overnight, typically 8 to 10 hours, at 64 to 68°F (18 to 20°C).

Step 5: The next morning, the dough will have doubled in size with a smooth surface. Place the bowl of dough, covered and untouched, in the fridge for at least an hour. The dough will firm up and become easier to work with later. You can use the dough after an hour, or leave it in the fridge for up to 24 hours, or until you want to make your pitas.

When you are ready to make the pitas, take the dough from the fridge and turn it out onto a floured surface. Using a dough knife, cut the dough into ten pieces, as equal as you can get by eye, or weighed out to 54 grams (2 oz) each, and shape each piece into a ball. Using a rolling pin, roll each ball into a thin, flat 6-inch (15-cm)-long oval. The dough will want to bounce back so you may need to leave it to rest for a few minutes before rolling it again.

Step 6: Place one piece of oval dough into the bottom of your air fryer basket. Turn up the heat to 400°F (200°C). Cook the shaped dough for 6 to 7 minutes on one side, then turn it over and cook it for a further 4 minutes on the other side, or until it is fully puffed and slightly browned. Repeat this to cook the rest of the pieces. Place the hot puffed-up pitas on a rack to cool and serve them immediately or store them in an airtight container for use later.

Top Tips: If you roll the pieces of dough too thin, they will not puff up and open into pockets; they will become perfect flat-breads instead.

The breads will come out of the air fryer crunchy and puffed up. They can be used immediately, or if you leave them to cool, they will soften.

To oven bake: Decide whether you would like to bake them in a preheated oven or from a cold start. If preheating, set the oven to 425°F (220°C) convection or 450°F (230°C) conventional. Place the pitas on a baking sheet. If you preheated the oven, bake them uncovered for 5 minutes, or until they are puffed up and starting to brown slightly. To bake them from a cold start, place the baking sheet in the oven, set the temperature as directed and bake them uncovered for a total of 7 minutes, or until they are puffed up and only slightly browning. Once they are baked, remove the pitas from the oven and eat them once they are slightly cooled.

Acknowledgments

Once again, I send the biggest thank you to my amazing editor, Sarah Monroe, from Page Street Publishing. Thank you for being open to the concept of this book, for being my guiding hand all the way through the process and for becoming my friend. You steer me perfectly and you make it all the more enjoyable for sharing it with me. And thank you to the entire team at Page Street, to Will Kiester for giving me these opportunities, to Meg Baskis for the brilliant book design, to Charlotte Lyman for your fabulous PR input and to everyone in the company for all your hard work. I feel very lucky to be a part of the Page Street family.

To my brilliant photographer, James Kennedy, I thoroughly enjoyed working with you again on this book. I LOVE all the photos. Thank you for letting me get involved with the styling of the shots, and for eating so much bread!

A massive thank you to White Lake Cheeses for sending me a selection of your brilliant cheeses and whey, and to Sally Prosser from the food blog My Custard Pie for being my cheese guide. Thank you to Anne Iarchy for the dough-braiding training, and to everyone at FWP Matthews Cotswold Flours for your support, sharing and friendships, especially Bertie, Emily, Sophie and Jenny. Thank you to the special people at *delicious.* magazine in the U.K. for always supporting me, and to *Pastry Arts* magazine in the U.S. for featuring me and including me in your virtual baking summits.

To my amazing Facebook group moderators, Ulrike, Linda, Claire, Shana and Alan, I cannot ever thank you enough for the help you give me, and for your love and friendship. And to all my group members, your continued trust, belief and love never fails to make me so very proud and so happy. Keep tagging me in your loaves and bakes; I love seeing them.

To everyone who has ever sent me a message or email or any form of communication online or in person, just a massive thank you. You boost me and encourage me and let me know that I am getting it right. You inspire me daily with everything you create in your kitchens and you have helped me to know what people want from me and their sourdough baking.

Thank you to the brilliant Sally Newton from the food blog Bewitching Kitchen for always being there, for being such a special friend and for being my sounding board and my U.S. ingredients and baking tips guide. I love you, my sister. xx

Special thanks to all my special friends. I worry about missing anyone so I will not list names, but I do hope you know who you are.

And always always, my love and thanks goes to my husband, Graham, and my son, Ben, for your love and support. And to Bob for always being under my feet!

About the Author

Elaine Boddy is a food blogger, author, self-taught sourdough baker and teacher. Through her website, her books *The Sourdough Whisperer* and *Whole-Grain Sourdough at Home* and her many social media platforms, Elaine helps people all over the world successfully bake sourdough.

Elaine and her sourdough pursuits have been mentioned in *delicious.* magazine and featured in *Pastry Arts* magazine. She has taken part in baking summits, was interviewed for The Sourdough Podcast and has been named and quoted in many other publications online and in print. Elaine is a member of the esteemed Guild of Food Writers.

Elaine lives in a small village in England with her husband, son and Bob the dog.

Index